BEST

WINTER WALKS AND HIKES
PUGET SOUND

BEST

WINTER WALKS AND HIKES
PUGET SOUND

HARVEY MANNING AND PENNY MANNING
Photography by Ira Spring

THE MOUNTAINEERS BOOKS

Published by
The Mountaineers Books
1001 SW Klickitat Way, Suite 201
Seattle, WA 98134

First edition, 1995, revised 1999. Second edition, 2002

Published simultaneously in Great Britain by Cordee, 3a DeMontfort Street, Leicester, England, LE1 7HD

Manufactured in the United States of America

Project Editor: Kerry Smith
Editor: Christine Clifton-Thornton
Cover Design: Kristy L. Welch
Book Design and Layout: Mayumi Thompson
Mapmaker: Jim Miller/Fennana Design
Cover photograph: *Mount Baker–Snoqualmie National Forest.* © Pat O'Hara
Frontispiece: *Early autumn snow*

Library of Congress Cataloging-in-Publication Data
Manning, Harvey.
  Winter walks and hikes in Puget Sound / by Harvey Manning ; photographs by Ira Spring.— 2nd ed.
      p. cm.
Rev. ed. of: Walks & hikes in the foothills & lowlands around Puget Sound, c1995.
Includes bibliographical references (p.   ) and index.
  ISBN 0-89886-822-X (pbk.)
  1. Hiking—Washington (State)—Puget Sound Region—Guidebooks. 2. Puget Sound Region (Wash.)—Guidebooks. I. Spring, Ira. II. Manning, Harvey. Walks & hikes in the foothills & lowlands around Puget Sound. III. Title.
  GV199.42.W22 P837 2002
  796.5'1'097977—dc21
                                                            2002012638

To Leo Gallagher and the others of the 100 club members
who loaned The Mountaineers the funds to publish
Freedom of the Hills, which began all this.

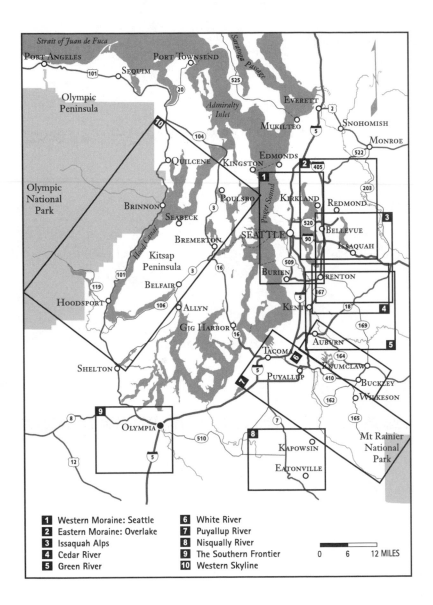

1 Western Moraine: Seattle
2 Eastern Moraine: Overlake
3 Issaquah Alps
4 Cedar River
5 Green River
6 White River
7 Puyallup River
8 Nisqually River
9 The Southern Frontier
10 Western Skyline

0   6   12 MILES

CONTENTS

INTRODUCTION

Trails. *True* trails. That is to say, trails for feet. The definition may be extended, where fitting, to include the hooves of horses and the paws of dogs. The wild things obviously are always welcome, whatever their means of locomotion, whether walking, hopping, flying, or squirming on the belly. They can be trusted to take care of their own manner

Coyote tracks in fresh snow

11

of motion. Our audience here is human. Trail-walking, that's the subject of this book.

However, as our faithful readers over the past third of a century have learned, we do not do books purely or even primarily to serve recreation. Re-creation ranks higher. Highest of all is preservation—preservation of those attributes which support the human claim to be superior to the sludgeworm, of those qualities which permit us to claim for Mother Nature superiority to a dump of sludge. It pleases us that our books have serendipitous value as guides to the kinetic-esthetic pleasures of walking. However, they really are something less and something more: pamphlets, broadsides, wall posters, political manifestos. To readers' complaints that they want directions on where to go, not lessons in how to behave, we answer, "If you don't want sermons, don't go to church." To those who disagree with our politics, we say, "Publish your own books."

A peroration may be in order telling how we got where we are. To start the story somewhere this side of the Big Bang and the Garden of Eden, in 1960, when the Climbing Committee concluded a five-year effort with publication of *Mountaineering: The Freedom of the Hills*, financed not by the impoverished club but by loans from club members who expected never to be more than partly repaid, we were startled by the commercial success. We had thought there were only hundreds of us climbers, never dreamt (nightmared?) thousands and, before long, tens of thousands. The profits (which were a conversion to cash of the unpaid labors of a hundred writers, reviewers, editors, and helpers) were an embarrassment. We saw them, too, as a danger, since they were all too likely to be exploited in ways that would fail to keep faith with us climber-volunteers, not to mention the quarter-century of the Climbing Course on whose experience the book was based. The Board of Trustees agreed and established the Literary Fund to receive income from and publish new editions of *Freedom* and to finance other books, including those that never would be undertaken by commercial publishers because by definition they would be furthering the purposes of The Mountaineers enunciated in 1906 and, thus, would very probably lose money.

To pass over the brothers and sisters, cousins and nieces and nephews of *Freedom*, in 1964 Tom Miller brought to a meeting of the Literary Fund Committee (the LFC, our unpaid, volunteer directorship) an English guidebook, which served as our model for *100 Hikes in Western Washington*. This epochal volume, published in 1966, was the first guidebook ever to top the Seattle bestseller list. It begat a half-dozen successors in our *100 Hikes* series and golly knows how many imitators across the nation.

The original plan of the LFC was for a book that would sample every manner of Mountaineers pedestrianism not entailing three-point suspension and rope and dynamic belay. We quickly saw, however, that the University of Washington Arboretum would not be displayed to proper advantage side by side with the Hoh River rain forest. Yet to publish walking books that failed to honor the arboretum was to deny an essential of our club heritage.

As chance would have it, the *Seattle Times* Sunday magazine was just then paying the first journalistic attention to walking any of us ever had seen. We recruited the author of these "Footloose in Seattle" articles, Janice Krenmayr, and in 1969 published her *Footloose Around Puget Sound: 100 Walks on Beaches, Lowlands, and Foothills.* A federal official addressing a national conference on the subject of urban and urban-edge outdoor recreation held up a copy of Janice's book and declared, "Every city in the nation should have a book like this." Before long, just about every city did.

Janice revised the book several times before being drawn to other enthusiasms. Having been her editor, I loved *Footloose* as dearly as if it were my own and couldn't endure watching it slip away. One thing led to another. From the spring of 1976 to the fall of 1978, I walked some 3000 "extra" miles, over and above normal backpacks in the high country and on the ocean beaches and exercises in my backyard Issaquah Alps. Between the front ridges of the Olympics and front ridges of the Cascades, on beaches, lowlands, foothills from Bellingham to Olympia, were born the "Sons of Footloose," the four volumes of *Footsore: Walks and Hikes Around Puget Sound.*

Revisions, new editions, more thousands of miles, and suddenly it was the 1990s and a decision from the Bottom Line to put to death the *Footsores.*

The execution has been only partly fatal. From the ashes rose, phoenix-like, the "Sons of Footsore." The 1993 *Hiking the Mountains to Sound Greenway* rescued the Snoqualmie Valley portion of the defunct *Footsore 2.* The 1995 *Walks and Hikes on the Beaches Around Puget Sound* assembled all the saltwater shores of *F-1, F-3,* and *F-4.* That left in limbo the large inland residue of the four volumes, to be covered by the single volume here in hand.

In 1976 I had set out for a comfortably finite updating of Janice's book. But as a few hundred miles of walking grew into a thousand, then two, and at last three thousand, I was gripped by an obsessive compulsion. My resolve became to comprehensively inventory the entirety of "the wildness within," to set forth a trails-preserving agenda for the citizenry and government. Periodic front-to-back revisions over the years kept the inventory reasonably current.

The political agenda is now even more urgent as we run out of open space, as every remaining patch of green is eyed by dollar-greedy trammelers. More surveyors are needed to publicize threatened lands and water. More publishers free from the tyranny of the Bottom Line. More amateurs.

If not a comprehensive inventory, this book is a useful sampling, an outline of what needs to be inventoried by a new legion of volunteer amateurs who ask no more than a little gas money and now and then a bit of peanut butter to spread on their crackers.

Until that legion does its work, we advise walkers not to throw out their *Footsores*. We implore librarians not to junk old editions. Move them to the History Shelf. The changes in lands and waters reflected in the editions since 1977 of the four volumes, and since 1969 of good old *Footloose*, are a uniquely valuable record.

> *This is the song that doesn't end,*
> *Yes, it goes on and on, my friend.*
> *Some people started singing it,*
> *Not knowing what it was,*
> *And they'll continue singing it forever just because*
> *This is the song that doesn't end . . .*
> —Shari Lewis and Lamb Chop

"IN WILDNESS IS THE PRESERVATION OF THE WORLD"
So says Henry Thoreau.

The Wilderness Act of 1964 defines a *national wilderness* as a place where "the Earth and its community of life are untrammeled by man, where man himself is a visitor who does not remain." Such places lie far from the likes of Walden Pond, they are "the wildness without."

Thoreau's Walden Pond was "the wildness within," swept around by civilization but not swallowed up. A *regional wilderness* has the size and/or topography to mask or mute the sights and sounds of civilization; if trammeled it can, over time, obscure a civilized past. A *community wilderness* has buffering that softens the rumble-bang-howl-honk-jangle—if it

South Prairie Creek

is carefully reserved for non-kinetic re-creations. A *neighborhood wilderness* lets a person hear the birds.

"It may be the love of wilderness that finally teaches us civilized responsibility." So says Wallace Stegner.

IN TRAILS IS THE PRESERVATION OF WILDNESS

"To make the world larger, go slower." So says me.

The *Oxford English Dictionary* defines "road" as "any way, path, or ordinary line of communication . . . wide enough to admit passage of vehicles." *OED* cites a passage from *Britain Under the Saxons*: "Every Coast and Part of the Land were miserably made the open rodes of spoyle and sackage."

The central distinction in our time between "road" and "trail" is speed. The "high road" from Edinburgh to London was traveled by "flying coaches" until they were replaced by the rail road. On the Oregon Trail the oxen drew wagons to the New Jerusalem but most of the pilgrims walked. Packhorses plodded the Cariboo Trail to the northern gold but the miners mainly traveled shank's mare. Feet went south from German forests to sack Rome, into Darkest Africa to find Dr. Livingstone, through snowdrifts to the one-room schoolhouse on the prairie.

But the world was too enormous for a person afoot ever to come in sight of the dragons at its edge, much less the gold and silver and precious jewels they hoarded. Trails had to be widened and groomed for wheels. Muscles of man and beast had to be augmented by mechanical advantage, then replaced by engines.

Medieval Christendom prayed through the year in a procession of saints' days; America celebrates the advent of summer with the Indianapolis 500. As soon as a child is able to walk he is taught to forget how, is equipped with wheels to commence training for adulthood on the freeways.

The anthros who clambered down from trees to the open savannah had to be quick afoot to elude the lions and tigers and bears. The genes of their descendants remember. The four-minute mile symbolizes the difference between reaching a tree and not.

Yet the long, long trail is still a-winding through memory to the land of sweet dreams. Freeway speed smells of blood, is as exciting as football, as war. The trail takes the measured pace of the feet in poetry.

A "trail" has been (since the fifteenth century, says *OED*) "a rude path or track beaten by human passage through a wild or uninhabited land." The transport of goods to market required something better, and so it came about that in its very first session the legislature of Washington appropriated funds for a Cascade Pass Wagon Road.

The National Park Service, created during the brash youth of the automobile, was inspired by the vision of bringing every temple of nature in easy view from the merry Oldsmobile. Though the youth failed to mature beyond brashness, the ruined vision of the rangers lingered on in their mocking "motor nature trails." Maps of the U.S. Geological Survey modernized the "wagon road" and "stock driveway" to "jeep trail." Maps of the U.S. Forest Service advanced the multiple-use that in the 1950s was set in concrete orthodoxy by promoting the old "stock trail" (for hooves and feet) to "4WD trail" or "ATV trail."

Such neologisms may be excused as accidental if oxymoronic linguistic perversions. But they are not accidental; they are cleverly deliberate. The perverters are not morons, they are artful exploiters, well-drilled in the lessons of advertising and politics. They know that if a thing is called by the wrong name over and over again, it can be accepted as its exact opposite. To put it another way, if a bad thing is repeatedly intermingled with a good thing, bad and good will be assumed to be two sides of the same coin. The "spoyle and sackage" can be equated in the public mind with goin' o'er the fields and through the woods to Grandmother's house.

A current and prominent example is the abuse of "bicycle trail." There is no walker so fanatically devoted to his preferred method of locomotion that he/she does not enthusiastically cheer the vehicle that promises to be an important element of a Soft Path solution to the automobile crisis. However, walkers are deeply offended by partisans of the wheel who in their enthusiasm muddle denotations by hijacking the happy connotations of "Bicycle Sunday" and "Daisy Daisy." There is no need. A "trail" is destroyed by an inundation of wheels as completely and surely as the fondly recalled "Sunday afternoon drive in the country" is by a 70 mph freeway. This is not open to debate. That's the way of it. The pity is that the estrangement caused by scramble-brained, flapping-lip wheel freaks is unnecessary. The happy connotations can be retained by rigorous use of "bikeway" and "bicycle path" rather than "bicycle trail," by preserving the precise denotations distinguishing "wheelways" from "footways."

Denotations were malevolently fuzzied and connotations wickedly sloppied by the Multiple-Use Acts that the U.S. Forest Service got Congress to pass in a fruitless attempt to forestall the Wilderness Bill, which in 1964 became the Act. Again, the villains of the linguistic piece have been the connotations. In a nation where "this land is your land, this land is my land," "multiple use" is the marching song of fairness, justice, and wisdom—the New Deal. As a comprehensive policy embracing an entire forest, a complete inventory of national resources, it is surely a fine song to march to. The Devil is, of course, in the details, in the calculated implementation. The slow and quiet and inexpensive cannot survive in a mob of the fast and loud and costly. The reality of a "multi-use trail" is "bikeway," serving as a foot trail only on rainy Tuesday mornings in February.

As the volume of nonmotorized travel has grown, the profession of highway engineer has been supplemented in college curricula by that of trail engineer. The construction methodology is appropriately adapted, but not the project goals, which are to move the most units at the highest speeds. Parks departments now adopt trail plans drafted by trail engineers (to draw back the curtain, bikeway engineers) who follow the philosophy of Social Darwinism, which is to dump all the cats in a gunnysack and let them fight it out.

There can be—and indeed must be—such a thing as a *motorfree multi-use travelway*. Service roads in the backcountry (forest management, utility lines), if gated to exclude public automobiles and motorcycles, can be amicably shared by foot, hoof, and bicycle. In urban-suburban areas where traffic is heavy and public open space at a premium, travel modes can be kept apart by barriers: walkers and wheelchairs in one lane, horses in another, and, in a third, bicycles and rollerskates and skateboards and scooters and joggers and runners. The separation is based not on a method of travel but speed.

PRIORITIES OF THE WITHIN

First, preservation. Of the world, for its own sake. Of the wildness, for the sake of the wholeness of the life community. Not for man apart.

Second, re-creation. "A city operates at high pressure in close quarters—it's the hot steam of the boiler room that blasts out the great ideas that *are* civilization. However, too much heat boils the brains. Only by providing getaway space for a quick and easy cooling off can a city keep on cooking."

Third—and only third—recreation. Genes of the great apes (and little monkeys) demand space for baseball and bullyball, tennis and golf. Further, the megalopolis needs a nexus of bikeways as extensive as that of motorways. Together with workable public transit, these are life-or-death to a city. They are, as well, recreational amenities.

Recreation vs. re-creation? Active vs. passive? Heavy impact vs. low impact? There's no "vs." about it. Willy-nilly, this is a multiple-use planet. Nevertheless, rose gardens are not planted in a football field, nor is basketball played in a concert hall.

Walking is the least impactful human use of a wildland—next to sitting on a log—which is bettered by not being in the wildland at all, as in watching whales on television rather than from a chase boat.

Feet do not have the odor of sanctity. Sitting on a log, motionless and silent, the human body has *some* impact. Too many bodies on too many logs becomes too much impact. Set feet and mouth in motion and impact grows. Jogging on trails is tolerable only in such places, at such hours, on such firm tread, as will not disturb the

Mount Ranier from The Divide

birdwatching and communing. Running on trails is an act of war. The bellow that destroys the lone walker's reverie ("TO YOUR REAR!" or "ON YOUR LEFT!") may be thought of as a courtesy. Not so. It is a warrior's command declaring the supremacy of the fast. So be it at the Olympic Games. On trails the slow rules. When passing an obstruction, the runner must become a polite and quiet walker. If not, the walker has the right of appeal. That's what the quarterstaff is for.

Neither are trails the paths to beatification. They always are invasions of wildness by civilization. To be sure, we enjoy walking them. They are "guilty pleasures" that can be justified by their role in making friends for wildness and recruiting its defenders, especially by green-bonding newcomers who require an easier introduction than plunging into a thorny thicket.

Volunteer militias have become hyperactive in building and maintaining trails, and that is good not only for keeping the devil's club from clawing our faces but as a potent political strategy. We must, however, accept the reality that just as the Crusaders gained evil reputations for plundering and raping their way to the Holy Land, our modern saints who come marching in their hardhat-haloes are not invariably doing the Lord's work. They may unwittingly be serving the Other.

Whenever building a new trail or resurrecting an old one, the volunteer must ask, "Does this task serve any purpose other than getting me in the front row of the choir?" Before ever taking up brush-hook or chainsaw, he/she must obtain a biologist's assessment of the impact of a new intrusion of civilization on wildlife livability. All reputable outdoor organizations engaged in volunteer trail work are now requiring approval of projects by the manager of the lands involved—if and only if that manager has the knowledge and the soul required. Increasingly our land managers do.

An emerging and important field of volunteer activism is not building but destroying trails. Many of those built in the last few decades have been designed as political statements. When the political goal is achieved, the builders then consult with the managers/biologists and obliterate lanes that have served their political purpose and should better be restored to wildlife refuges. A great many trails date back to the era of forest management by means of fire lookouts, backcountry ranger stations, and backcountry telephone systems. Many of these are still, as always, treasured re-creational, recreational, green-bonding routes and are maintained. Others have long since been forgotten and overgrown but have recently been rediscovered on old maps and proposed for restoration. In some cases the trails deserve rebirth. In many others the reversion to wildness is welcome and volunteers (and managers) should respect Nature's decision.

THE CONSPIRACY

The Other also has a choir. Sir Thomas More, Lord Chancellor of England until he lost his head, wrote in *Utopia*, "So God help me, I can perceive nothing but a conspiracy of rich men procuring their own commodities under the name and title of a Commonwealth."

That was 1516. So what else is new? During the Great Barbecue of the public domain of America in the nineteenth century, powerful bandits corrupted Congress and boldly stole—in Washington State alone—an empire larger than all but the major nations of Europe. The Populists of the turn of the century who cried out for revestment of the Northern Pacific Land Grant were mostly out-at-the-elbows dirt farmers who spoke English with a foreign accent. They weren't heard when American money talked. (So what else is new?)

My first intimations of the conspiracy came in the 1960s, at a meeting of academics, Forest Service officers, and heirs of the Big Steal to discuss recreation on forestlands east of Seattle. An academic dwelt on the fact that the lands closest to Seattle, and thus most useful for mass recreation, were scarcely used at all because they were Land Grant legacy, privately owned, undeveloped. A Weyerhaeuser spokesman responded that to develop the lands would be an expense that could not produce income and thus a profit, because free recreation was provided just a little farther from the city by the Forest Service. Said he, "Charge admission to your lands and we can to ours."

The thought was so preposterous it instantly fled my memory—until the 1990s, when Weyerhaeuser, following the example of Champion International on the Kapowsin Tree Farm, installed tollgates on entries to its road system.

Bit by bit, very gradually, the conspiracy emerged from the think tanks, and as it took solid form, was seen by those few who looked into the shadows of Washington, D.C., to be, indisputably, a Conspiracy. The master plan commonly is credited to Derrick Crandall, president of the American Recreation Coalition, whose members are in the business of selling recreation, or, as it is becoming better known, "wreckreation." The campaign advanced on two fronts. In Congress, those who devoutly, even rabidly advocate the deconstruction of

Deschutes Falls

government to give the free market the opportunity to do the job better, have been systematically starving the U.S. Forest Service and National Park Service; any hiker crawling over fallen trees can testify to the success. In the forests, the managers plead poverty and their cries for relief are answered (by the Scrooges of Congress) by the Fee

Demonstration Program, implemented in our area by the Northwest Forest Pass. And lo! Weyerhaeuser installs tollgates. Onward, gathering momentum, rolls the bandwagon. Washington State Parks begins charging walkers for parking at trailheads. Observers long in the tooth recall a question famously asked at an Easter Day parade in 1933: "I wonder what the poor people are doing today?"

Wreckreation proceeds. The forest rangers are sincere, their hearts truly bleed, they agonize over their inability to serve the public as has been their tradition. They are deeply hurt by the growing antagonism of their good ol' buddies, the hikers, who now view Smokey Bear as a cop, and not a genial cop. Many hikers do not see a Conspiracy, see out-at-the-elbows rangers brushing away tears, and feel that a person who lays out a hundred bucks for boots and ten bucks for gas to the trailhead shouldn't mind paying five bucks to park here, five bucks to park there, five bucks to park anywhere. They do not object because they are not distressed by the tip of the iceberg, fail to realize there is more to it than that, more that will be revealed as privatization of public lands goes on, and on. Those hikers who are combating the Conspiracy, who refuse to buy a Forest Pass, as Henry Thoreau refused to pay the poll tax that paid for the Mexican War, become contemptuous of their good ol' buddies of the trail who have no more brains than a lemming.

Hostility in the wildlands, that's not the least of the collateral damage being done by the Northwest Forest Pass, the nose of the camel snuffling under the wall of the tent.

MANAGERS OF THE TRAILS

For each of the hiking areas in this book, the principal land manager is named. Few of the lands herein are federal, and those agencies will therefore not be characterized. Two state agencies are prominent, Washington State Parks and the Department of Natural Resources. My experience with both has been that the hands-on field managers tend to be of good minds and especially good hearts, doubtless because they have their hands mainly busy on the land, less on papers shuffling across the desk. Fortunately, goodness frequently leads to promotion, and their hearts often are able to resist the effects of office air. Not always, and the higher they rise, the more distant the aroma of the woods, the more powerful the attraction of high places. That is to say, politics. In State Parks and the DNR I have known splendid people, though not always as splendid as they would be if there were not, higher than them, officials who are not splendid at all or just don't care.

As an example, when the fat-tire bike appeared on our trails, I witnessed State Parks officials attempting to rein in the conquistadorism and being overruled in Olympia. By whom? I don't know my way around Olympia well enough to speculate.

My experience is more complete with the DNR. Under Ol' King Cole the agency was known as the worst of all possible land managers. When he was toppled by the Revolution of 1980, it became, in my Issaquah Alps experience, the best of all possible managers. However, even in those Twenty Fat Years that followed 1980, I learned to my sorrow that goodness at the top, in Olympia, could carry on down to the likes of the Issaquah Alps only if there were a strong citizen involvement. In earlier editions of this guidebook (and its *Footsore* predecessors) I strove with might and main to help Olympia goodness filter down to the Capitol State Forest, the Tahuya State Forest, the Ahtanum Multiple-Use Area, the Reiter Razzerland. No use. The Old Regime was too deeply entrenched in local politics. Then came the Restoration Election of 2000 and I have given up on lost causes—lost to me, though not to the doughtier champions that must come.

The parks departments of counties and cities are in some cases well known to me and admired or not according to individual cases. The larger the governmental unit and the parks department the more difficult for goodness to triumph over political careerism, but it does happen, glory be, and I will not risk the successes by bestowing dangerous compliments.

There are those who declare that any piece of land larger than can be overflown by a single flight of an arrow is not fully private, and if it gives rise to rivers, or harbors wildlife, or has (or did have) forests that were 10,000 years in establishing themselves in the glacial moraines, can be nothing other than public, or at least must be managed in the light of the Public Trust Doctrine, as opposed to the Private Greed Doctrine exemplified by the Northern Pacific Land Grab.

In earlier books I sought to bring the private forests within my inventory. However, in this book my only coverage of the Kapowsin Tree Farm is how a walker can sneak past the tollbooth. The ill-gotten Weyerhaeuser hoard is barely mentioned, and only the unguarded back doors. My energies formerly devoted to making the best of a crooked deal will now be diverted to the campaign to revest the land grant, to repeal the Great Barbecue.

A NEW PLAYER IN THE GREAT GAME

The previous paragraph, written at the start of 2002, will be let stand as background to the January 16 collision of two tectonic plates—the Public Trust of Environmentalism and the Private Greed of Robber Baronism. The shuddering was right off the high end of the Richter scale. My seismograph broke. Not to analyze in detail but to starkly report:

The Evergreen Forest Trust, a non-profit conservation company, has agreed to purchase from Weyerhaeuser 104,000 acres of the Snoqualmie Tree Farm, a major chunk of the 900,000 acres that Frederick Weyerhaeuser acquired from Jim Hill in 1900 for $6 an acre. The money, $185,000,000, will be obtained by selling Community Forest Bonds, a new concept.

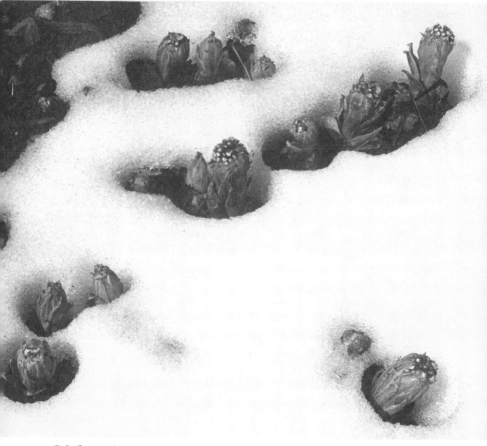

Coltsfoot pushing through last winters snow

Logging will continue, perhaps on the model of Tiger Mountain State Forest, a genuine multiple use, a true sustained yield. As on Tiger, sensitive areas will never hear chainsaws again. Ecological preserves comprising about a tenth of the total will include two major rivers (North Fork Snoqualmie and Tolt), smaller streams (such as Griffin and Tokul Creeks), more than 500 acres of lakes and ponds, 6000 riparian acres, and more than 4000 acres of wetlands.

The specter of Puget Sound City sprawling eastward to the Cascades will at last be dispelled. Developers and highwaymen will have a stop. Wildlife can carry on. The forest industry will continue to have a guaranteed base in the low elevations where trees grow big, fast.

This edition will not resurrect such favorites of the old *Footsores* from Griffin Marsh to the Black Canyon, the Tolt Forks to Fuller Mountain. The management plan for the Evergreen Forest will be a while in preparation. We can afford to wait; no guidebook pamphleteering is required to save the old favorites. They are saved.

Weyerhaeuser still holds 1,400,000 acres in Washington, including the White River Tree Farm on and around Mount Rainier. Dare we hope for more good news? Weyerhaeuser has 30,000,000 acres in North America and golly knows how many in South America, Indonesia, and Siberia. Enough, we think.

ON THE TRAIL

John Fremont devoted the years from 1842 to 1846 to his Great Reconnaissance of the Rocky Mountains. From 1976 to 1978 my Volkswagen beetle rolled over better than 80,000 miles to trailheads between Bellingham and Tenino, the Cascade front and the Olympic front. My non-motorized feet plodded 3000 miles. New editions followed, more years, more miles. Much has happened since then, for good and ill. More books have appeared, some niche-fillers, others more or less egregious cream-skimmers, and a few, notably those by Ken Wilcox, joining the efforts of Ira Spring and me in preaching up a crusade. There even are regular, even superb, newspaper columns, recalling how amazed we hikers were, in the late 1960s, when Janice Krenmayr pioneered in giving attention to feet with her "Footloose in Seattle" series in the *Seattle Times*. Finally, outdoor organizations that once devoted their entire preservation effort to the "wildness without" have extended their concerns to the "wildness within." Also, up and down the Puget Trough there are new organizations—the "Friends of This," the "Friends of That." Bless them all.

In this new millennium, therefore, I retreat from my Fremont-scale inventory to selectivity. My partner, Ira Spring, employs the term "green-bonding" for the systematic nurturing of the newcomer to the ways of the wilds. I address not all the good walking there is, to stir up politicking for preservation, but only enough good walking to help imbed the love of wildness in the psyches. Another form of politicking, of course.

To do a bit of blatant marketing, I've amended the title to stress the "year around," which I always thought was self-evident, but apparently not to everyone. I have, in hike descriptions, provided highest elevations attained. Any height less than 2500 feet or so can dependably be hiked in just about any winter except those of an Ice Age. (Incidentally, there is new evidence suggesting that global warming may not be our only worry, the Earth may be on the brink of Pleistocene II.) The trips herein of elevations higher than 1000 to 1500 or so feet should be kept in mind when the kids want to throw snowballs and there's no raw material in the yard. Dogs love to roll around in fresh fluff and there is fun for adults in "postholing." The sport of "snowline-probing" is an excellent alternative to crowding yo-yo hills of the Cascade passes.

The subject here is day-hiking, no overnighting, and I regret that fact because green-bonding is not complete without the nights, the stars in the sky, the rain on the tent, the things that creep and crawl and those that go bump. But where, close to home and safe from marauding criminals and suspicious police, do troops of Boy Scouts or Girl Scouts go to experience, nowadays, the wild of night? Ask the nearest scoutmaster/scoutmistress.

Many books feature "Nature" in their titles, and bully. Few pages herein are not full of it. Mall-walking is not my game.

Information given in trip descriptions on number of miles and feet of elevation gained is useful for folks with young kids or elderly parents when choosing trips suitable for them.

Trails designed to accommodate the handicapped are at present far too few and are not noted here. Many "multi-use trails" are paved and level and serve wheelchairs well, though of course not without the disturbance by swift wheels. Are there in our vicinity any self-guiding sightless trails? I don't know of any.

"Walks" are short, on gentle paths, in forgiving terrain, requiring no special clothing other than what one would wear to go out of the house, and no experience other than ability to distinguish right foot from left and operate them in sequence.

"Hikes" are longer and/or rougher, have enough ups to require some huffing and enough downs to twist an unwary ankle. The feet need stout shoes or boots, the body needs clothing to bar the chill winds and shed some of the rain. A rucksack is essential to carry the Ten Essentials, which aid routefinding and cope with emergencies. These are:

1. Extra clothing—enough so that if a sunny-warm morning yields to a rainy-windy afternoon, or if an accident keeps the party out overnight, hypothermia will not threaten.
2. Extra food—enough so something is left over at the planned trip end, in case the actual end is next day.
3. Sunglasses—if travel on snow for more than a few minutes may be involved.
4. Knife—for first aid and emergency firebuilding (making kindling).
5. Firestarter—a candle or chemical fuel for starting a fire with wet wood.
6. First-aid kit.
7. Matches—in a waterproof container.
8. Flashlight—with extra bulb and batteries.
9. Map.
10. Compass.

A word about maps: For each section of this book the U.S. Geological Survey maps are noted. Better for the hiker are the Green Trails versions, where the private publisher puts green overprints and other information on USGS base maps to show current roads and trails. The maps in this book are provided for general orientation but are not sufficient for travel navigation.

A word about driving directions: It is assumed here that anyone driving to a trailhead has in the glove compartment the highway maps for the state and street maps for the boroughs of Puget Sound City. Directions are given for roads where they become complicated near the trailhead but not for how to get the car out of your garage.

A word about garbage: What you can carry in full, you can carry out empty. Take back to the trailhead every can, candy wrapper, foil, orange peel, and tissue.

A word about water: For a day hike, fill your canteen at home. Since you won't wish to build a fire to give wild water the required ten-minute boil, carry iodine treatment (Potable Aqua or other) to ward off the dreaded giardiasis (the Boy Scout trots).

A word about the alimentary: Yes, the new method dictated by the needs for mob sanitation takes some getting used to. Please do. When body wastes cannot be internally retained to a trailhead or home toilet, place them for rucksack carrying in doubled, heavy-duty, sealable plastic bags.

A word about safety: That a trail is in this book does not guarantee it will be safe for you. The route may have changed since the description herein. Creeks flood. Gravity pulls down trees and rocks. Brush grows up. The weather changes from season to season, day to day, hour to hour. Winds blow, rain soaks, lightning strikes, the sun sets, temperature drops, snow falls, avalanches happen.

This book cannot guarantee that you are safe for the trail. Strength and agility vary from person to person. You vary from decade to decade, year to year, day to day, morning to afternoon to dark and stormy night.

You can reduce backcountry risks by being informed, equipped, and alert, and by recognizing hazards and respecting your limits. However, you cannot eliminate risk, and neither can the authors, or The Mountaineers, or the attorney hired by your next of kin. It's a dangerous world out there. Perhaps you'd be happier as an armchair adventurer. But you may wish to strap yourself in as a precaution against earthquakes.

—Harvey Manning

A NOTE ABOUT SAFETY FROM THE MOUNTAINEERS BOOKS
Safety is an important concern in all outdoor activities. No guidebook can alert you to every hazard or anticipate the limitations of every reader. Therefore, the descriptions of roads, trails, routes, and natural features in this book are not representations that a particular place or excursion will be safe for your party. When you follow any of the routes described in this book, you assume responsibility for your own safety. Under normal conditions, such excursions require the usual attention to traffic, road and trail conditions, weather, terrain, the capabilities of your party, and other factors. Because many of the lands in this book are subject to development and/or change of ownership, conditions may have changed since this book was written and may make your use of some of these routes unwise. Always check for current conditions, obey posted private property signs, and avoid confrontations with property owners or managers. Keeping informed on current conditions and exercising common sense are the keys to a safe, enjoyable outing.

Opposite: *Japanese garden in Washington Park Arboretum*

THE WESTERN MORAINE: SEATTLE

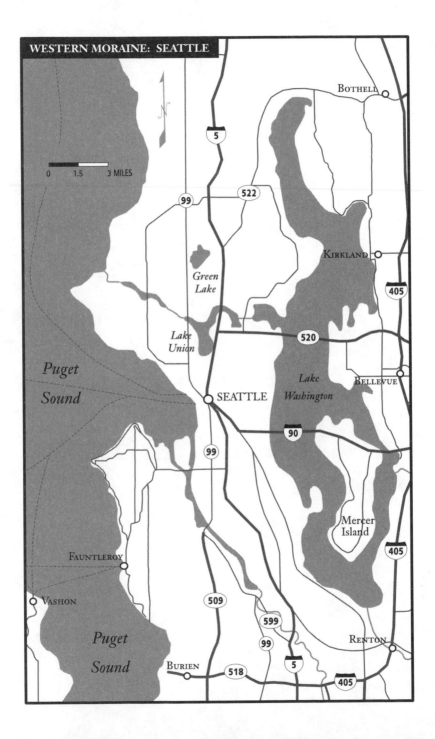

WESTERN MORAINE: SEATTLE

THE WESTERN MORAINE: SEATTLE

Management: Seattle Parks Department
Topographic maps: USGS Edmonds East, Seattle North, Kirkland, Shilshole Bay, Seattle South, Mercer Island—and their equivalents in the Green Trails series, privately published

To the pioneer boomers, it was "New Rome on its Seven Hills," none rising as high as 500 feet. Later, it became the "Queen City," then the "Emerald City," and now the core of "Puget Sound City," pent between The Whulge ("the saltwater we know") and the Big Water (Lake Washington).

Seattle is urban to the hilt, but threaded through with green, and every walkway reachable sans automobile—trips done solely by bus and foot.

In 1884, the Seattle park system was founded upon a donation of 5 acres by David and Louise Denny. "Park" then, and for years after, meant lawns and gardens for strolling, benches for sitting, always dressed in Sunday best. There wasn't much call for "walking," not in an era when everybody got enough of *that* on the way to catch the streetcar or steamer, nor for preserves of "wilderness," when plenty of *that* lay at the ends of streetcar lines and handy to steamer docks across the water.

"Trolley car parks" became popular for picnic socials of schools, Swedes, and refugees from North Dakota. "Electric parks" dated from the Midway at the 1893 Chicago World's Fair, and by World War I drew throngs of fun-seekers to be dazzled and thrilled. Luna Park was near Alki Point, and White City Amusement Park adjoined Madrona Park, which with Leschi Park was owned by the Seattle Electric Company until Seattle acquired the streetcars and with them the parks.

Dunlop's invention of the pneumatic tire in 1888 set off the great American bicycle craze; Seattle's street engineer, George Cotterill, responded with a system of bike paths. Whether the machine was built for two or one, Daisy did indeed look sweet upon the seat. Every fine Sunday was a Bicycle Sunday for young and old. Starting from Cotterill's system, in 1903 John and Frederick Olmsted, sons of the Frederick Law Olmsted who designed New York's Central Park, proposed a network of scenic boulevards, "emerald necklaces strung with play-grounds and parks" within a half-mile of every residence in the city. "An ideal system," they told the City Council, "would involve taking all the borders of the different bodies of water, except such as are needed for commerce, and (enlarging) these fringes . . . so as to include considerable bodies of woodland as well as some fairly level land, which can be cleared and covered with grass for field sports and for the enjoyment of meadow scenery." In the Olmsted philosophy, "Civilization can't thrive in the absence of fresh air and green, open spaces" that preserve the "good and wholesome" environment of the country within the city.

Extension of city trolley lines created the "interurbans" and, with them, the distant recreation sites of "trolley car tourism." But then, as the adolescent city grew toward an adulthood of green ganglia threading through a flesh of residential and commercial wood and brick and concrete, there slithered into incipient Eden the serpent—or better say, bounced and honked and backfired, disguised as the Tin Lizzie, the Merry Oldsmobile, the Buick and Plymouth and Chevy. The "tin can tourists" converted wagon roads to highways. The Sunday walk in the park and bike along the boulevard yielded to the drive in the country. Picnics shifted to Lake Wilderness and Lake Serene, Flaming Geyser and Green River Gorge, Snoqualmie Falls and Maloney's Grove, and—incredibly to those who in less than a decade lived from Model T to Model A to V-8—Paradise Valley.

A glorious party it was, it was, a stupendous half-century binge. Then Seattle awoke. With a terrible hangover. The jug of cheap gas was empty. The nearby countryside had been filled overnight by new cities. The farther countryside was receding behind freeways clogged by mobs of cars, the emerging nightmare of gridlock. For quick and easy getaways, Seattle of 1970 had to stay home—in a park system admirably suited to 1910.

In the 1960s a civic realization dawned that R. H. Thomson, revered as "Seattle's Engineer," was the Great Beast who had stolen Seattle's soul. In 1968 a Great Awakening of born-again Olmsteders approved King County's Forward Thrust, a bond issue to provide funds for parks. In 1972 the Army, short of ready cash to fight the war in Southeast Asia, dumped surplus land which was snapped up to become Discovery Park. In 1977 the Navy similarly unloaded what became Sand Point Park. Also in the 1970s, Burlington-Northern abandoned a rail line, which became one of the most-used urban trails in the nation, the Burke-Gilman.

All in all, it was a decade that pious Greens cherish as the Second Coming of the Olmsteds. To a chorus of praising and clapping, in

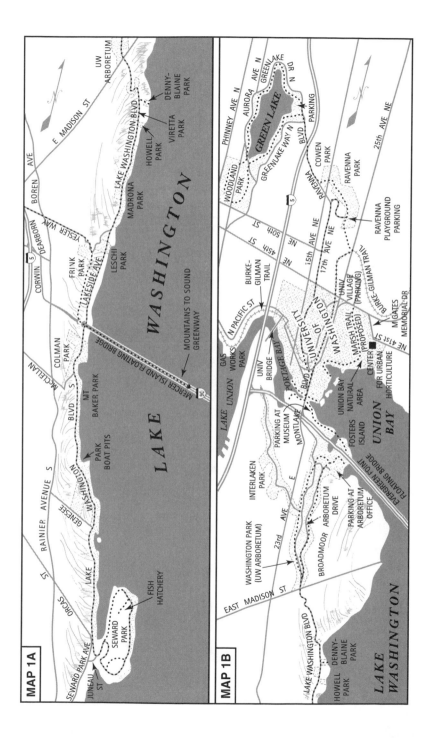

MAP 1A

UW ARBORETUM

DENNY-BLAINE PARK

E MADISON ST

LAKE WASHINGTON BLVD

VIRETTA PARK

HOWELL PARK

BOREN AVE

MADRONA PARK

YESLER WAY

DEARBORN

CORWIN

FRINK PARK

LESCHI PARK

LAKESIDE AVE

MCCLELLAN

COLMAN PARK

LAKE WASHINGTON

MERCER ISLAND FLOATING BRIDGE

MT BAKER PARK

S BLVD

LAKE WASHINGTON

MOUNTAINS TO SOUND GREENWAY

PARK BOAT PITS

RAINIER AVENUE S

GENESEE ST

ORCAS ST

SEWARD PARK AVE

JUNEAU ST

FISH HATCHERY

SEWARD PARK

MAP 1B

PHINNEY AVE N

AURORA AVE N

GREEN LAKE DR N

GREEN LAKE

PARKING

WOODLAND PARK

GREENLAKE WAY N

BLVD

COWEN PARK

RAVENNA PARK

25th AVE NE

RAVENNA PARK

RAVENNA PLAYGROUND PARKING

NE 50th ST

NE 45th ST

15th AVE NE

17th AVE NE

BURKE-GILMAN TRAIL

N PACIFIC ST

BURKE-GILMAN TRAIL

UNIV VILLAGE (PARKING)

BURKE-GILMAN TRAIL

UNIVERSITY OF WASHINGTON

M GATES MEMORIAL DR

NE 41st ST

GAS WORKS PARK

LAKE UNION

UNIV BRIDGE

PORTAGE BAY

BLVD

MARSH TRAIL (PROPOSED)

CENTER FOR URBAN HORTICULTURE

MONTLAKE

PARKING AT MUSEUM

INTERLAKEN PARK

E

UNION BAY NATURAL AREA

FOSTERS ISLAND

UNION BAY

WASHINGTON PARK (UW ARBORETUM)

23rd AVE

BROADMOOR

ARBORETUM DRIVE

PARKING AT ARBORETUM OFFICE

EAST MADISON ST

EVERGREEN POINT FLOATING BRIDGE

LAKE WASHINGTON BLVD

HOWELL PARK

DENNY-BLAINE PARK

LAKE WASHINGTON

1977, an Urban Greenbelt Plan was adopted by the Seattle City Council. But there then sprang up from a lurking in dark slimes of the human spirit the Serpent God, and it was déjà vu all over again.

Not quite. Some civic leaders had learned a lesson and had taken it to heart. When in 1979 the original proposal was made for what became the Cougar Mountain Regional Wildland Park, "wilderness on the Metro 210," the first government official to publicly express support was the mayor of Seattle.

OLMSTED WAY

One way: 18½ miles
High point: 300 feet
Elevation gain: 400 feet
Maps: 1A, 1B

To New York City, "Olmsted" means Central Park, and to the nation, the National Park Act, and to Seattle, the Lake Washington Boulevard, the grand entrance to the Alaska–Yukon–Pacific Exposition staged in 1909 on the University of Washington campus. The 1916 lowering by 10 feet of Lake Washington, preparatory to the next year's opening of the Lake Washington Ship Canal, added a strip of new

Madison Park and Lake Washington

lakeshore land, as had the 1911 lowering of Green Lake for no good reason except to make new land.

The Seattle citizen who wishes to know his/her city in the intimate way never possible atop or within a machine ought at least once to do the whole 18½ Olmsted miles at a single go. Thus the eyes feel through the feet the connectedness of kempt lawns, wild marsh, an arboretum of native and exotic plants, a forest, and three lakes.

Directions: *Leave the car at East Green Lake. Ride three buses, one at a time, to Seward Park.*

Walk back to Green Lake, sustained in rain or blisters by knowing that ever close by to abbreviate the 18½ miles is Metro.

SEWARD PARK

Round trip: 4½ miles
Map: 1A

Directions: *Seward Park is on the western shore of Lake Washington, south of the I-90 bridge, and is accessed via Lake Washington Boulevard South. Start at the entrance to the park, just off the boulevard at Juneau.*

The Olmsted Way, done scrupulously, begins by looping around Bailey Peninsula, formerly an island. Fish hatchery, fishing piers, bathing beaches, and views to Rainier.

Lake Washington's trough was gouged by the Canadian glacier which on the most recent of several visits arrived hereabouts some 15,000 years ago and left 13,500 years ago, at the Seattle-area maximum heaping 4000 feet thick. The lake's greatest depth is 205–210 feet. The water level ranges between 20 and 21.85 feet above the mean low tide of the saltwater. Primevally, the lake's sole major tributary was the Sammamish River, though in flood time some of the Cedar River spilled in through the marshes. The outlet was the Black River, which joined the Cedar River in the Renton vicinity to enter the Green River, the union of waters changing name to Duwamish River for the final stretch to Elliott Bay. To keep floodwaters of the Cedar from drowning cows in Allentown and Georgetown, the stream was diverted into Lake Washington, becoming its second major tributary and its only source of pure high-Cascades water. Metro's good deed of shunting sewage from the lake deserves only half the credit for keeping the shore suitable for trophy homes; forgotten when the medals are issued are the cow-milkers of Allentown and clean waters of the Cedar.

The lakeshore is the number-two attraction of 278-acre Seward Park. Number one is the path through Seattle's largest ancient forest, close to 1 mile in length and averaging ¼ mile wide.

WASHINGTON PARK ARBORETUM

Round trip: 1 mile or 4
Maps: 1A, 1B

Directions: *Start at Madison Playground, along Lake Washington Boulevard or Arboretum Drive, or at the north Broadmoor entrance.*

The 7-odd miles north from Seward Park connect a string of parks. Madison, Leschi, and Madrona were emplaced in the early 1890s to

Canoeing in an Arboretum waterway

stimulate purchase of adjoining lots, platted by street-railway companies. The Olmsted Plan added Mount Baker, Colman, and Frink. Leschi was, prior to the semi-Floating Bridge, the landing for ferries to Mercer Island and Bellevue, close by the terminus of the cable car over the hill from Yesler Way. Trails climb the wildwoods past mysterious bulks of ancient concrete. A springtime glory of rhododendron blooms in a plantation long since gone wild, and very nicely so.

The Mountain to Sound Greenway crosses the Big Water via I-90. The Olmsted proceeds through Howell, Viretta, and Denny-Blaine Parks to the University of Washington Arboretum in 200-acre Washington Park, thousands of trees and shrubs from the world over, artful landscaping of ridges and valleys, marshes and ponds and creeks. The Arboretum needs to be visited plant by plant, one end to the other, along Lake Washington Boulevard, Arboretum Drive (Upper Road) on the ridge east of the valley, and valley-bottom Azalea Way. When these tours are finished it's another season and the whole job has to be done over.

FOSTER'S ISLAND–WATERFRONT TRAIL–MONTLAKE BRIDGE

One way: 1½ miles
Map: 1B

Directions: *Start at the north Broadmoor entrance or the Museum of History and Industry (2700 24th Avenue East).*

The Evergreen Point (Albert D. Rosellini) Floating (for now) Bridge and its plotted connections to a chimerical R. H. Thomson Expressway ripped off a fifth of the Arboretum-that-used-to-be, brutalized Foster's Island, drearied the marshes of Union Bay. The havoc would have been worse had not the Save the Arboretum campaign of the early 1960s driven a stake through the heart of Seattle's Quintessential Engineer, a man high on the dishonor rolls of the city's Hall of Shame for flushing Denny Hill into Elliott Bay and ramming a sewer through Magnolia Bluff to West Point.

From the north Broadmoor parking lot the path crosses a slough to Foster's Island. Groves of water-loving trees. Sails on Union Bay. The Cascade horizon. From the island the Waterfront Trail crosses a marsh that is not primeval, formed as it was after the lake was lowered. "Never mind," says the wildlife, "it *feels* primeval." Cottonwoods

The route weaves out through head-high thickets of hardback to what would be open water were it not for lily pads.

and willows, cattails and horsetails and bulrushes. Mammals from mice to muskrats. Beavers with a tooth out for tender young saplings. An estimated 100,000 birds a year, visiting or nesting or miscegenating. Partly a floating walkway, partly a spongy lane of cedar chips atop floating mats of peat, the route weaves out through head-high thickets of hardback to what would be open water were it not for lily pads, passes observation platforms and benches for sitting and reflecting. Jogging is banned; the posted speed limit is 1 mile per hour. The Waterfront Trail ends at the Museum of History and Industry, to which the city sacrificed a delicious little park in precisely a spot that cried out most piteously for a delicious little park.

The walking continues without a break on the Lake Washington Ship Canal Waterside Trail, which rounds the corner to the Montlake Cut, connecting Union Bay of Lake Washington to Portage Bay of Lake Union. Before climbing steps to picturesque Montlake Bridge, built in 1925 and doing a nice job even now in humbling hasty hordes of automobiles, sidetrip ¼ mile west to a parklet at the end of the cut. Fine view over the Seattle Yacht Club to Lake Union. The lake's maximum depth is 50 feet. Due to filling and building, its area is only half the primeval, and half of that is covered with boats and houseboats and other Privatizers of the Public Domain.

UNIVERSITY OF WASHINGTON CAMPUS 👟

Round trip: 4 years
Map: 1B

Directions: *The University of Washington can be reached from I-5 by taking the 45 Street exit east, just north of downtown Seattle. Limited parking can be found on many streets near campus. If you park farther afield, the Burke-Gilman Trail gives easy walking access to the campus along NE Pacific Street and Montlake Boulevard NE.*

Pause while crossing the Montlake Bridge to muse. Primarily, the marshes of Union Bay seeped water to Portage Bay. In 1861 Mr. Harvey I. Pike set to work with pick, shovel, and wheelbarrow to dig a ditch joining the lakes. There wasn't much call for it at the time.

University of Washington campus

However, in 1883 Messrs. Denny, Burke & Company hired Chinese laborers to deepen the channel to float sawmill-bound logs through the marsh to a flume emptying into Portage Bay. In 1899 a band of farmers dynamited the canal, hoping to lower Lake Washington in a "whoosh!" and save their pastures from spring floods of the Black and Cedar Rivers. In 1916 the U.S. Army completed the task begun by Pike, though the Montlake Cut wasn't tidied up until 1921.

Before proceeding to the central campus, sidetrip from the bridge along the waterside path, an extension of the Arboretum Trail designed to give close but respectful views of wildlife. When Lake Washington was lowered, 610 acres of Union Bay became marsh. For decades Seattle dumped and burned household garbage here, the University complacently expecting to ultimately gain a new East Campus. The 1960s discovery that the garbage and underlying peat would be generating methane gas for many centuries to come, making any structure a potential bomb, forced the former lake/marsh to be permanently dedicated to parking lots. An outer 55 acres, though, was preserved from blacktop as the Union Bay Natural Annex surrounding the Center for

The rest is a pond-studded grassland fringed by marsh, a permanent refuge for travelers on foot or wing.

Urban Horticulture. About 20 acres are gardens, research plots, and (well-ventilated) greenhouses and classrooms. The rest is a pond-studded grassland fringed by marsh, a permanent refuge for travelers on foot or wing.

The central campus is worth a few hours or years. Time lacking, the quickest way to Ravenna Park is 1½ miles on the Burke-Gilman Trail to Ravenna Playground.

RAVENNA PARK

One way: 1 mile
Map: 1B

Directions: *Start at the Ravenna Park playground, at NE Ravenna Boulevard and NE Park Road.*

Cars cross the bridge and never know the park is in the gulch beneath. A walker in the gulch, beside the creek under the big firs and maples, is scarcely aware of the tumult above. In the late 1880s Reverend and Mrs. William W. Beck bought the ravine and nurtured a park named for the town in Italy, which was the final home of Dante. Ravenna Creek then was a large stream, full of trout, flowing in the open from Green Lake to Lake Washington. The Becks built paths, waterfalls, a music pavilion. In 1902, the 25-cent admission fee was gladly paid by 10,000 visitors. The Becks named ancient Douglas firs in honor of Paderewski and assorted local politicians. The tallest, some 400 feet, was Robert E. Lee. The one with the largest girth was Teddy Roosevelt, who on a visit affirmed it was, indeed, a "big stick."

In 1911 Seattle acquired the park by condemnation in order to condemn Ravenna Creek to the nether regions of Thomson's North Trunk Sewer. Clarence Bagley's 1929 history described the park as a "dark, dank, dismal hole in the ground." In the 1930s the city logged the park. The site of the Roosevelt Tree is now a tennis court.

Even so, the trees not mill-worthy in the timber-glutted 1930s are now 70 years closer to ancience and the ravine has quite a virgin-forest look. The Ravenna Creek Alliance proposes to daylight the creek, resurrecting it from the depths to again flow in the open to Lake Washington. Why not? Birds don't fly through sewers.

GREEN LAKE

Circuit: 2.8 or 3.2 miles
Map: 1B

Start anywhere around the shore.

At the urging of W. D. Wood, a settler-promoter who in the 1890s had joined two companions in building the Green Lake Circle Railroad loop around the lake and up from the Fremont streetcar line, in 1911 Seattle purchased Green Lake and lowered it 7 feet to expose hundreds of acres for use as park, streets, and sundry civic

Green Lake's multiple-use trail

> *The time for serenity at Green Lake is in a misty dawn, alone.*

purposes. More of the lake was destroyed by filling—the last of the dirt coming in 1932 from the big ditch dug for Aurora Avenue through Woodland Park. Now a mere 260 acres, the lake has a maximum depth of 29 feet and is in so advanced a state of eutrophication that at any season after early summer and before the fall rains, swimmers routinely contract the "Green Lake crud." Seattle City Water used to help keep the lake clean by flushing in surplus drinking water; nowadays, though, there isn't much surplus. Walkers are safe so long as they don't touch the water.

The attractions of Green Lake (lawns and trees, views of surrounding ridges and Rainier, mobs of resident and migratory waterfowl, who have their own sanctuary, Swan or Duck Island) need little praise. On a single summer day, as many as 10,000 people visit the park, and as many as 1000 an hour take to the paths—the 2.8-mile interior path (10 feet wide) near the shore and the 3.2-mile outer path near the streets. Some 29 percent walk, 26 percent rollerskate, 46 percent bicycle or jog or run. There also are skateboards and baby strollers, and, as fast as they burst from the fevered imaginations of diseased chimpanzees, every other wheeled device that serves as an argument for nuclear winter.

Fewer pedestrians come to walk the trail than to sit in a safe refuge and, as at a hockey game, enjoy the Sabbath violence. One is reminded of New York's Central Park, which until assignment of police reinforcements was a charming springtime spot to watch the young lovers mugging the old lovers. The time for serenity at Green Lake is in a misty dawn, alone.

WOODLAND PARK

Perimeter loop: 2 miles
Map: 1B

Directions: *Start along Phinney Avenue North.*

Adjacency to parks sells building lots. Thus, in 1891, developer Guy Carleton Phinney built a hotel, dance pavilion, boathouse (on Green Lake), shooting lodge, and woodland trails affordable by folks unable to go on safari with The Mountaineers—"wilderness on the trolley line"—the Green Lake Electric Railway (the Olmsteds hated it).

In 1899 Seattle bought the park and civilized it with rose gardens, a zoo, playfields, picnic tables, and, eventually and temporarily, a campground for tin-can tourists. In 1912 the North Trunk Highway was completed from 85th Street, Seattle's city limits, to the Snohomish County line. Paving and "improving" culminated in a 1930s re-routing through Woodland Park. In 1932 a swath of ancient forest, then Seattle's largest (thus the name "Woodland"), was clearcut and a ditch dug through the stumps for "The Great Aurora Highway," named not, as is often ignorantly supposed, for taking a straight aim on the North Pole but for the Illinois hometown of Dr. Kilbourne, a Seattle dentist. On May 14, 1933, the masses turned out with flags and orations and whistles to cheer the grand opening. What did commuters gain in addition to saving 1000 feet of driving the park-skirting alternative proposed by the Olmsteds? Editorialized the *Seattle Times*, "A reminder at least twice a day that you sacrificed Woodland Park."

The bifurcated remnant teaches us that the evil done by engi-

Grizzly bear in Woodland Park Zoo

neers lives after them. Yet at certain hours of certain days of certain seasons the park, among Seattle's largest, can give miles of lonesome strolling. My favorite used to be the middle of a heavily snowing night.

BURKE-GILMAN ONCE AND FUTURE TRAIL

One way: 21 miles
High point: 100 feet
Elevation gain: minimal
Maps: 2A, 2B

While a student living in an old millworkers' lodgings by Lake Union, just below tracks of the railroad built by Judge Thomas Burke and Daniel Gilman and fellow townboomers, I often walked the line to the university campus, on the way home picking up spilled coal for my cookstove.

In the late 1960s, by then a university hireling, I was initiated into a conspiracy to latch onto the right-of-way about to be abandoned by the Burlington-Northern. Also by then being founder-director (unpaid) of The Mountaineers Books, I recruited Janice Krenmayr to write *Footloose Around Puget Sound* and in it to include the proposed trail. Thus in October 1969 came the first public revelation of what she referred to as an "oughter be" trail: "Railroad—Canal Locks to Woodinville." In 1973, Burlington-Northern, Seattle, the university, and King County having done their duties, she was able to include the Burke-Gilman Trail in her "Lake Washington Loop, a 51-mile route."

Janice ultimately proceeded to other adventures and I formally adopted the orphan. In 1977 I parked my VW beetle at the university, walked to Bothell, caught the bus back to campus, and in *Footsore 1* hailed the creation of "one of America's great urban trails . . . an inspiration for the nation."

So it was, and so it can be again—once separated by wheel-barring barriers from one of America's great urban bikeways. Tragically, wheel-spinners unborn when the hiker-biker cabal was conspiring treat walkers now as trespassers. Pedestrians who refuse to slink away whimpering have begun carrying, in the horizontal, cross-body position, the 6-foot quarterstaff that served Little John and Friar Tuck so well. A dour historian would cite this as illustrating that war never brings peace, only a new war. But this, too, shall pass, because the

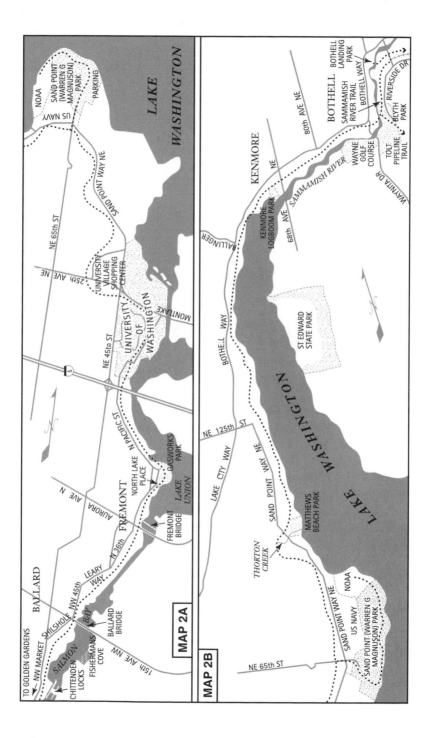

MAP 2A

TO GOLDEN GARDENS
NW MARKET
BALLARD
SHILSHOLE NW 45th
FISHERMANS COVE
SALMON BAY
CHITTENDEN LOCKS
15th AVE NW
BALLARD BRIDGE
LEARY WAY
N 36th
AURORA AVE N
FREMONT
FREMONT BRIDGE
N PACIFIC ST
NORTH LAKE PLACE
GASWORKS PARK
LAKE UNION
NE 45th ST
5
UNIVERSITY OF WASHINGTON
MONTLAKE
NE 65th ST
25th AVE NE
UNIVERSITY VILLAGE SHOPPING CENTER
SAND POINT WAY NE
US NAVY
NOAA
SAND POINT (WARREN G MAGNUSON) PARK
PARKING
LAKE WASHINGTON

MAP 2B

LAKE WASHINGTON
KENMORE
80th AVE NE
NE
BALLINGER
KENMORE LOGBOOM PARK
68th AVE
SAMMAMISH RIVER
WAYNE GOLF COURSE
BOTHELL
SAMMAMISH RIVER TRAIL
BOTHELL WAY
BOTHELL LANDING PARK
RIVERSIDE DR
BLYTH PARK
WAYNITA DR
TOLT PIPELINE TRAIL
BOTHE.L WAY
ST EDWARD STATE PARK
NE 125th ST
LAKE CITY WAY
SAND POINT WAY NE
THORTON CREEK
MATTHEWS BEACH PARK
SAND POINT WAY NE
NOAA
US NAVY
SAND POINT (WARREN G MAGNUSON) PARK
NE 65th ST

Burke-Gilman Trail

hearts both of walkers and wheelers are, more often than not, pure. Side-by-side, barrier-separated trails and bikeways ultimately will make all the saints happy.

GOLDEN GARDENS PARK TO GASWORKS PARK

One way: 6 miles
Map: 2A

Directions: *Golden Gardens Park looks out to Puget Sound from the north-western shore of Ballard and is reached from the south via Seaview Avenue NW, along Shilshole Bay.*

Golden Gardens Park is sufficiently praised in our companion book, *Walks and Hikes on the Beaches Around Puget Sound.* Meadow Point is Seattle's sole surviving intact spit, complete beach: driftwood line, dune line, even a bit of lagoon. No swimming pools, sewage plants, aquariums, or beach-invading bulkheads. A popular bathing beach since 1907 as a private development, the 95 acres were acquired for the public in 1923.

The 1 mile to Chittenden Locks has fine views over a jetty sheltering googols of dollars worth of playboats to Puget Sound and the Olympics.

The most entertaining walking on the Burke-Gilman is where it doesn't yet officially exist and perhaps never will, on the old rail grade. The honest industrial grime of Seattle's only old-style working waterfront is easily enjoyed by the walker, whose pace allows friendly relations with heavy machinery.

Watching vessels in Chittenden Locks, find idle amusement by mentally preparing the Environmental Impact Statement for a project bragged up of yore as one of the Seven Wonders of Seattle. Consider, for example, the impact if the closure system failed totally, as it has partly on more than one occasion. A wall of water up to 12 feet high, depending on the stage of the tide, would burst from Lake Washington to Shilshole Bay. Lake Washington would drop, in an estimated 80 hours, to the level of Puget Sound. The tides during the estimated eight months required for repairs would forbid use of the floating bridges, assuming they did not collapse, as is likely. Barges stuck in the mud. Playboats stranded in marinas. The front yards of software tycoons stinking something dreadful.

The 1¼ miles from the locks to Ballard Bridge feature houseboats, fishing boats, and the little freighters that serve the North— *Pribiloff, Silver Clipper, Polar Merchant*. Across the tracks is Old Ballard, restored and revived and full of red bricks and lutefisk. Climb the stairway to the bridge for views west out Salmon Bay to the locks and east to the Fremont Cut.

The 1¾ miles to the Fremont Bridge start with more ships *(Trident, North Sea, Orion)* and views to Queen Anne Hill. After a dull inland mile the tracks return to the water at Canal Street and pass Fremont Canal Park. Where a creek used to flow from Lake Union to Salmon Bay is the Fremont Cut, paths and poplars on both banks, ships and boats and canoes and ducks passing to and fro. On Friday the 13th, March 1914, a dam at this point, erected to exempt Lake Union from tidal flow, burst, sending a deluge to Ballard and beyond. Industry preempts the shore the final scant mile to the Fremont Bridge.

Tour the Fremont District, site of a mill founded in 1888 by four speculators, two from Fremont, Nebraska. A successor, Burke Millwork, was still operating in 1946, when I worked as helper on a planer and in that pre-earplugs era learned a rudimentary sign language while getting well along toward becoming deaf as a shingleweaver. The reason for a town at this point was the outlet creek of Lake Union, which permitted easy bridging in 1887 by the Seattle, Lakeshore & Eastern Railroad, six years before Jim Hill brought his Great Northern rails in from the north. By 1890 electric trolleys were speeding to and from Ballard along a timber trestle at 20 miles per hour; a couple of decades later my grandfather, fresh in from the Old Country (North Dakota), hired on as a conductor. In 1891 the town of Fremont was annexed by Seattle and in 1917 was termed its "geographical center."

The Fremont Bridge, successor to the timber span over "the creek," opened in 1917 to serve the Lake Washington Ship Canal. The handsome bascule structure is said to be the nation's most-opening bridge, about every ten minutes on a summer day, or 1600 times a year, or an estimated half-million times in its first sixty years (twice as many as the Ballard Bridge, also dating from 1917), letting through 100,000 vessels a year.

When Seattle learned funk, it painted the bridge blue and orange to befit the Fremont District, which had fallen into shabby decline after the 1932 opening of the Aurora Bridge on the brand-new Aurora Highway. During the history revival of the 1960s, the derelict storefronts were swabbed out and psychedelicly brightened. The key tourist attraction is Richard Beyer's sculpture, *Waiting for the Interurban*, a group of life-size figures whose neighbors garb them with sweaters in chill weather, put flowers in their hair in springtime, and set out bowls of dogfood for their best friend. At the base of the Aurora Bridge another artist-community cement sculpture depicts an enormous troll emerging from the cement in the act of devouring a real (but cemented over) VW Bug, said by reliable sources to be from California.

The 1½ miles from 3rd NW to Gasworks Park pass marinas, sailboats, fishing boats, and rusty old buckets kin to the one abandoned by Lord Jim.

GASWORKS PARK TO MATTHEWS BEACH PARK

One way: 7¼ miles
Map: 2A, 2B

Directions: *Gasworks Park is on the north shore of Lake Union, with parking on Northlake Way.*

Walkers wanting a quiet day safe from arrogant wheels stay within the confines of Gasworks Park. Inspect machinery of the plant which, for 50 years, starting in 1906, generated gas from coal dug in the Issaquah Alps and along the Green

Climb the grassy knoll for a view of downtown Seattle.

River. For its opening as a park in 1975, the buildings and metalwork were made children-safe and painted gay colors. Walk the ¼ mile of frontage path on Lake Union. Tugboats, sailboats, police boats. Climb the grassy knoll for a view of downtown Seattle. Gulls, ducks, coots, crows, pigeons.

The University of Washington campus? A book in itself. For this one, gaze out Rainier Vista to The Mountain and over Lake Washington to the Cascades. Then carry on past the largest natural area of the campus, the Bob Pyle Wilderness, named for the world-famous butterfly man who as a student led the resistance against another heap of bricks. Under the 45th Street viaduct the route leaves the campus to

Gasworks Park

curve around a former bay, now University Village, returning to lake views at Sand Point.

At Thornton Creek, the city's largest watershed and one of its three significant streams not banished to a Thomson sewer pipe, a path ascends past a Metro pumping station to a lake panorama. A wildwood greenery has been reconstructed by citizen volunteers of the Thornton Creek Alliance.

Another surcease from speeding wheels is Matthews Beach Park. Stroll in peace up the forest knoll and down the lawns in views over the waters to sails and mountains.

MATTHEWS BEACH PARK TO BLYTH PARK

One way: 8 miles
Map: 2B

Directions: *Matthews Beach Park is on the western shore of Lake Washington, north of the 520 bridge, and can be reached from Sand Point Way NE.*

Local folks may be seen afoot on dark and stormy nights and dawn constitutionals, but few visitors come from afar to walk the 3 miles of residential neighborhoods to the city limits, then 2½ miles by lakeside homes of Sheridan Beach and Lake Forest Park.

However, Logboom Park is a good-in-itself destination, reached via 61st Avenue NE off Bothell Way. Groves of cottonwood, willow, maple, and alder are isles of cool peace on summer days. The shore, mostly marsh-natural, is habitat for mallards, domestic white ducks, exotics originally from Asia, and weird hybrids. The concrete pier, located where rail cars once dumped logs from a timber dock to be "boomed up" in rafts for towing to the mills, gives views down Lake Washington and across a marina to the mouth of the Sammamish River.

In 1993 the Burke-Gilman was completed the 2½ miles through industrial Kenmore and by pastoral greenery of the river, which is crossed on a refurbished rail bridge to Blyth Park, 21 miles from Golden Gardens Park. Here the Burke-Gilman ends, the Tolt Pipeline and Sammamish River Trail begin.

The shore, is habitat for mallards, domestic white ducks, exotics originally from Asia, and weird hybrids.

SAND POINT (WARREN G. MAGNUSON) PARK

Round trip: 3 miles
High point: 50 feet
Elevation gain: none
Map: 2A

Directions: *Seattle's newest "superpark" (360 acres of "prime waterfront") is best reached on fine summer Sundays by walking ½ mile from the Burke-Gilman along NE 65th from Sand Point Way.*

Implementation of the twenty-year plan adopted in 2001 will attract hordes of cars into the park, three for every parking space. When this gift of the people to the U.S. Navy after World War I (for a seaplane base) was regifted to the people in the 1970s, thanks to Senator Maggie, it was the Oklahoma Land Rush all over again. The treaty that ended a quarter-century of uncivil war gave the soccer Nazis and kinetic allies lebensraum of a fifteen-field sports complex. Tennis got fourteen courts. Dogs (on leash) were granted 9 acres. Some 4 miles of "cross-country trails" (no speed limit). ("Run, Lola, run!")

The golden age of Sand Point for me was World War II, laboring in the "Boneyard." That is, I would have labored had there been anything to do, but there wasn't. Each morning I punched in, climbed a hill, now the designated kite-flying area, sat under a tree and read a book, napped, absorbed the view over the Big Water to the mountains, punched out, went home.

The long 1 mile from the south fence to the north fence is well worth a leisurely loiter. The ballet of the sailboards, a *pas de trois* of water, wind, and human. The birds, oh aye, the birds! I once spent an hour at a copse of willows on the shore, property of a pair of redwing blackbirds. A great blue heron flew slowly by, then picked up the pace under attack by the nest-guarder, who menaced and squawked the suspected chick-molester all the way across Lake Washington, and on returning took off after a circling hawk, and then me.

Adjoining the park on the north is the NOAA boundary, home port of its ocean-graphing Great White Fleet. The Rover Boys have ameliorated their preemption of intended parkland by providing 2000 feet of waterfront walking that features basalt chairs and tables, pedestrian bridges inscribed with texts from *Moby Dick*, and a "sand garden" constructed of pipes.

Children's play area in Sand Point Park

OTHER TRIPS

Beacon Ridge. A 200-foot-wide, broad-view powerline swath, horses grazing, roosters crowing. Country in city much of the 5 miles from Jefferson Park to Skyway Park.

Greenbelts. In 1977 an Urban Greenbelt Plan proposed fourteen areas for preservation. A Beacon Hill Greenbelt Trail has been roughly pioneered from Dr. Jose P. Rizal Park to 13 Avenue S, a one-way distance of 1¼ miles to near the start of the Beacon Hill powerline lawn. Citizens are planning ecosystem restoration and interpretive paths for St. Mark's Greenbelt. In various stages, hampered by shortage of funds and an excess of greedhead speculators, are Southwest Queen Anne, Northeast Queen Anne, Duwamish Head, East Duwamish, East Duwamish–South Beacon Hill, and West Duwamish Greenbelts.

A greenbelt doesn't have to "do" anything. It serves by simply lying there making no noise (but soaking up a lot), polluting no air or water (but always cleaning), being looked at ("part of the urban fabric"), and being lived in (not by thee and me but by squirrels, rabbits, weasels, muskrats, raccoons, and beavers, and by red-tailed hawks, great blue herons, gulls, nighthawks, horned owls, screech owls, geese, jaegers, ducks, and grebes, and by moles, voles, mice, and rats, and by pigeons, wrens, and warblers, and by those sly old coyotes that everybody in the neighborhoods assumes are just plain dogs).

Creeks. The civilizing of the Western Moraine entailed getting the creeks out of sight, in storm sewers or basement-to-basement. The new age of uncivilizing wants to bring primeval creeks to the surface where fish can swim, birds sip, and pedestrians hum along with the naiads. Three significant streams escaped, partly or wholly, banishment to Hades by Engineer Thomson. The Thornton Creek Alliance is working to "open up" the headwaters (which developers call "ditch water") in the Northgate Shopping Center and "wild" the course to Lake Washington. Friends of Carkeek Park have largely achieved restoration of Pipers Creek. Community groups in West Seattle are proposing a 3-mile trail along Longfellow Creek past the West Seattle Golf Course to the Duwamish Waterways near Elliott Bay. The Ravenna Creek that flows through Ravenna Park is a mockery of the ancient, now buried, creek from Green Lake to Lake Washington; "daylighting" is sought. Citizen efforts are encouraged and abetted by Seattle's $4,500,000 Urban Creeks Legacy Program.

The Whulge (that is, Puget Sound and associated saltwaterways). Surely it is idiotic to do a book about Seattle walking and omit the entire saltwater shore of The Whulge (Lushootseed for "the saltwater we know"). Except, we have a whole other book as companion to this, *Walks and Hikes on the Beaches Around Puget Sound*. Described therein are the 20 crow-flying miles from Seattle's Duwamish Head to Tacoma's Browns Point, the 36 miles from the Skid Road to the site of the Everett Massacre, and the beaches and woodland trails of Dash Point State Park, Dumas Bay Wildlife Sanctuary, Poverty Bay Park, Redondo Park, Saltwater State Park, Des Moines Beach Park, Seahurst Park, Lincoln Park, Alki Beach Park, Myrtle Edwards Park, Discovery Park, Golden Gardens Park, Carkeek Park, and Richmond Beach Park, to mention only the most major parks.

Opposite: *Luther Burbank Park*

THE EASTERN MORAINES: OVERLAKE

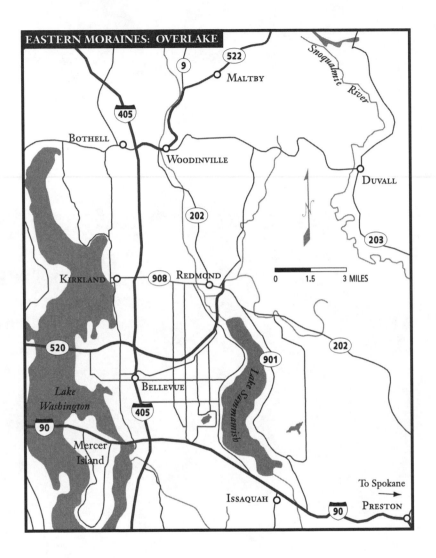

EASTERN MORAINES: OVERLAKE

522

9

MALTBY

405

BOTHELL

WOODINVILLE

DUVALL

202

203

N

0   1.5   3 MILES

KIRKLAND

908

REDMOND

520

202

901

Lake Sammamish

Lake
Washington

BELLEVUE

405

90

Mercer
Island

Snoqualmie River

To Spokane

ISSAQUAH

90

PRESTON

THE EASTERN MORAINES: OVERLAKE

Management: City parks departments, King County Parks, State Parks
Topographic maps: USGS Mercer Island, Bothell, Maltby, Kirkland, Redmond, Issaquah, Fall City—and their equivalents in the Green Trails series, privately published

The plateau of glacial debris and meltwater hydraulics west of the Big Water is paralleled by two others on the east. Will "Overlake City," the new borough of Puget Sound City now a-building, evolve a soul before an errant asteroid writes finis to this planet's business? The cacophony of what threatens to be the Final Gridlock is distracting. However, a fair start has been made on preserving greenlands for the feet.

Elevations range from near sea level to a bit more than 500 feet; except during ice ages and typhoons, the year-round weather never impedes the feet. Elevation gains are minor.

Luther Burbank Park

In melting away some 13,500 years ago, the Canadian glacier left the troughs of the Big Water and the Little Water, trisecting the moraines into three north–south highlands. They were in the condition of unorganization that geomorphologists call "infancy." Where had been coherent rivers from the glacier front now were lakes, marshes, swamps, and bogs connected by dribbles and seepage. The engineer cohorts of R. H. Thomson tidied up the landscape, put the water out of sight underground, civilized wetlands into real estate. After a century the Seattle moraine had a mere three significant streams on the surface, only the most major of lakes, and no bogs at all.

This sort of forced maturing was well advanced on the Bellevue–Kirkland moraine when a new word burst on the public like a rising star: ecology. The citizenry had been told that when living space was paved over the displaced wildlife would move in with relatives. Now it learned that every nook of nature is full up, no empty room for cousins. Destruction of habitat is destruction of critters. People tend to be fond of critters.

Thus it was that on the middle moraine the imprisoned creeks began to be set free and signs giving their names emplaced so they no longer could be dismissed by sneering developers as "ditchwater." Public opinion swung dramatically away from All Power to Private Property to Keep Bellevue Boggy.

The easternmost highland, East Sammamish Plateau, entered the 1980s very nearly in a state of grace. By the 1990s, however, the Private Greed Doctrine, formidable as the glacier from Canada, had come down like a wolf on the fold, biting and clawing for jawsful of gold.

LUTHER BURBANK PARK

Loop trip: 1½ miles
High point: 50 feet
Elevation gain: 20 feet
Map: 3

The 77-acre park on the north shore of Mercer Island has 300 feet of lakefront, and some 1½ miles of footpaths.

Directions: *Go off I-90 on Exit 7, Island Crest Way, turn onto 84 Avenue SE, and from it at SE 24 Street enter the park.*

Walk north from the headquarters building past a froggy cattail marsh to Calkins Point and views of the University District. Follow

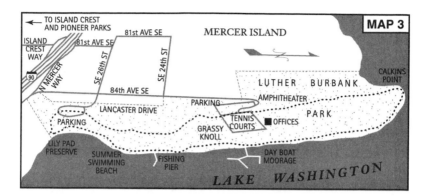

the shore south to views of the East Channel and Cougar Mountain, to the fishing pier, through madrona and Indian plum woods to the swimming beach and the marsh at the park border.

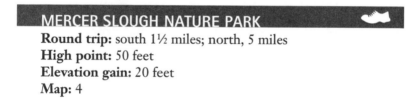

MERCER SLOUGH NATURE PARK

Round trip: south 1½ miles; north, 5 miles
High point: 50 feet
Elevation gain: 20 feet
Map: 4

The hand of man, wielding a shovel, lowered Lake Washington by 9 (10?) feet in 1916 (1917?), converting Mercer Bay to a slough and bog, and dug ditches to dry things up enough to grow garden truck. After opening of the Bellevue Shopping Square, the business and industry that loves flat land began running short of the dry variety and invaded the wet. However, to free developers from foreign (Seattle) meddling, a city was incorporated. That entailed a parks department, and more by luck than brains the city recruited a staff whose concern for bawfields was magnificently complemented by a love of the wet.

Thanks to eventual support by voters (it didn't come instantaneously) there now is the 326-acre Mercer Slough Nature Park, the largest urban wetland in the region, the largest wetland park of King County—and of the western United States. The sedges and rushes, willows and dogwoods shelter 168 of the 212 species of animals found in wetlands of the state, 104 species of birds.

Some 6 miles of nature trails (foot-only) and a 5.3-mile periphery bikeway hitch together viewpoints for watching beaver, herons,

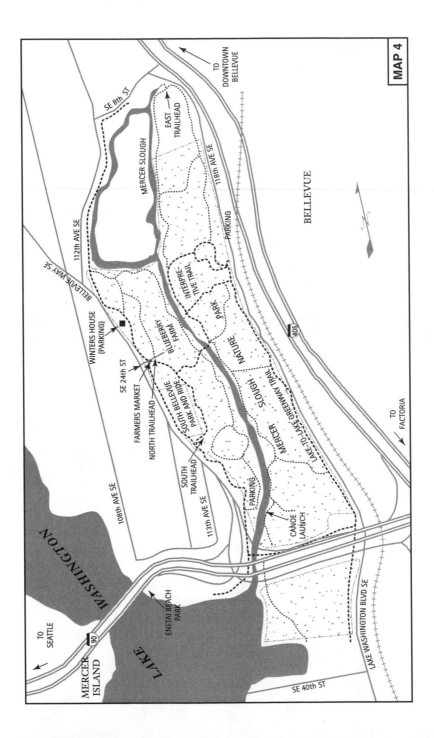

MAP 4

waterfowl, and whatever else that swims, flies, creeps, scurries, or burrows.

Directions: *The best of the three trailheads is on the south, at the interpretive center. Go off I-90 on Bellevue Way SE 0.2 mile to South Bellevue Park & Ride and a short path to the center site.*

South from the center, the bikeway: In a short bit is the T where the right heads for Enetai Beach Park; the side trip to that shore is worth a few minutes. The left parallels the massive concretery and hurling roar of I-90, surrealistic so cheek-by-jowl with cattails and flitting-swimming birds. The bridge arching gracefully over Mercer Slough is the pedestrian's proper turnaround after a look south to the gray geometry of freeway and down to the tea-colored water of the slough and north along the tantalizing alleyway hemmed in tight by impenetrable (not to critters) willow jungle.

North from the center: A reconstructed slough has been planted with native trees and shrubs. A boardwalk-trail turns east from the valley wall, far over what was, until 1917, the bottom of Lake Washington,

Bellefields Nature Park

The sedges and rushes, willows and dogwoods shelter 168 of the 212 species of animals found in wetlands of the state, 104 species of birds.

now a wetland willow jungle, cattail marsh, sphagnum bog, and squishy meadow. The tumult of I-90 is lost in that of I-405. Above the reeds loom, distant as a nightmare at noon, the towers of downtown Bellevue. At a Y a gravel path turns left to the Farmers Market at Overlake Blueberry Farm, a scant ½ mile from the center. From the Y the right fork is a long ramp through willow swamp and hardhack to a view platform on the banks of Mercer Slough. A pretty bridge crosses to Bellefields Nature Park. A ten-car parking space beside 118 Avenue SE is the start of a 1-mile loop trail. The sign "Bellefields Nature Park 1966" identifies it as the birthplace of the Bellevue Parks reclamation project. The path descends a bank to what was, until 1917, the shore of Lake Washington and enters a wildland only three-quarters of a century old (before that, it was wild water).

Turn south along Mercer Slough. Pass stubs to the tea water where, as a readerboard says, "bufflehead, goldeneye, wigeon, gadwall, merganser, and ruddy duck" pause for food and rest during migration and the year-rounders include "Canada geese, mallard, and great blue heron." The way leaves the slough for a mowed meadow, where stands a big old white-barked paper birch (native) as well as a big old lonesome blueberry bush (alien). The wood-chip path Ts with the ramp to The Bridge. Loop left back to 118th through lawn corridors and poplar groves. A reader board tells the sequence on a line at this place from west valley wall to east: shrub/scrub wetland, Overlake Blueberry Farm, Mercer Slough, meadow, forest, forest wetland, 118th.

LAKE-TO-LAKE GREENWAY TRAIL

One way: 7 miles
High point: 230 feet
Elevation gain: 200 feet
Map: 5A, 5B

Defensive incorporations by residential communities a-feared of being swallowed up and digested by the Shopping Square forced Bellevue to resign itself to being the "city between the lakes" rather

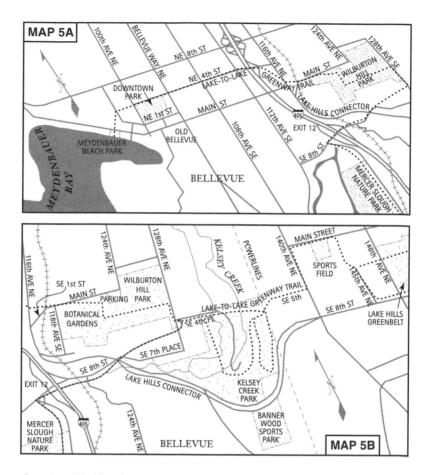

than (see Kirkland) a "city on a lake." Not to mind. Students of wild-life prefer, as does wildlife, a stew of muck, murk, and weedery. The 7 miles of the Lake-to-Lake Greenway Trail connect a necklace of small-to-middling parks. Several have walking that is worth the while, an hour or several for each stroll.

WILBURTON HILL PARK

Loop trip: 2 miles
Map: 5A

Directions: *Go off I-405 on Exit 12, turn east on SE 8 Street, and turn left at the stoplight onto Lake Hills Connector, which bends north to become*

116 Avenue NE. Turn east on SE 1 Street, over the railroad tracks. Turn right on Main Street to the Wilburton Hill parking lot.

The marvel is that a 103-acre chunk of country survived the construction all around it of the All-American Shopping Square City. It was snatched from the jaws of the blacktoppers in 1988, a triumph of the new, grown-up Bellevue. But then came a second civil war, between the contemplatives who treasured the hilltop, 230 feet, for its high and long views and no sounds louder than the wind, and the daddies and mommies in club sweaters who lusted to cheer the shrieks of their kinetic offspring as they kicked a baw and each other around a field of bloodied grass.

The bawfields won. At times (dawn) the contemplative can hear birds. The 2 miles of woodland paths are an amenity for neighbors, not worth a journey from very far.

But hold on! Don't leave the scene without walking the railroad tracks from SE 1st south to the Wilburton Trestle, a timberwork 948 feet long and 100 feet high at the center, built in 1904 and latterly provided a safe walkway. The rails still see the occasional train, running 22 miles from Black River Junction in Renton to Woodinville, a better walk than the Burke-Gilman because the iron wheels disturb the peace far less than some others.

KELSEY CREEK PARK

Loop trip: 2½ miles
Map: 5B

Directions: *Go off I-405 on Exit 12, turn east on SE 8 Street, cross Lake Hills Connector at a stoplight onto SE 7 Place, and drive via 128 Avenue SE and SE 4 Place into the park.*

That the agricultural past be not forgotten, and that children may know other animals than dogs and cats, this former farm has been revived, barns and pastures, cows, pigs, horses, burros, goats, and sheep. Another attraction of the 80-acre park is the Fraser House, a cabin of squared-off logs built nearby in 1888 and moved here to be preserved. There also are undeveloped natural areas, valley marshes, and hillside forests.

A figure-8 route looping around the edge of the bowl-shaped wetland, the creek's floodplain, combines the Farm Loop and the Hillside Loop for a 2½-mile total.

Barns and farm fields at Kelsey Creek Park

LAKE HILLS GREENBELT PARK

Round trip: 3 miles
Maps: 5B, 6

The Original Inhabitants rendezvoused here to pick the fall crop of native blueberries and cranberries in the bogs and marshes bordering "Lake Primeval," draining northward to Kelsey Creek. The Originals having been departed, a homesteader dug a ditch to drain the waters to Lake Sammamish. The old lake shrank to two remnants, Phantom and Larsen. Ove and Mary Larsen came from Denmark in 1852, homesteaded at "Blueberry Lake" in 1889, combining farming (they sold wild cranberries and blueberries in Seattle) with his job in the Newcastle mines. Other immigrants, from Japan, began farming hereabouts in the early 1900s. In 1918 the Larsens sold 80 acres to the four Aries brothers, who ran the area's largest farm, shipping carrots, celery, peas, lettuce, cauliflower, potatoes, cabbage, and parsnips to Montana, Minnesota, and the Yukon. In 1947 Louis Weinzirl planted domesticated blueberries. In 1960, K-Mart rolled out the blacktop. (Thus we have been taught by Bellevue's great historian, the late Lucile McDonald.)

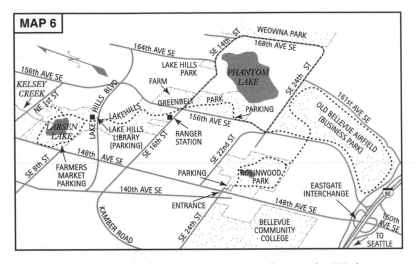

Of the 8-mile wetland once continuous from Lake Washington to Eastgate, the middle 2½ miles between Kelsey Creek Park and Larsen Lake went the age-old way of drying-up and building-up. But the preservation instincts of Bellevue Parks gained a powerful supporter, the Storm and Surface Water Department, which had learned the cheapest way to get its assigned task done is to let Nature do it. The Urban Wildlife Enhancement Project converts monoculture of hardhack spirea to diverse habitat of pond, wetland, dry land, woodland, and vegetation, which provides food, water, shelter, and living space for wildlife. Duckweed, soft rush, yellow iris, reed, canary grass, salmonberry, and forest filter storm water runoff.

Of the Greenbelt Park's 154 acres of land and 17 acres of lake, only 2 percent will be developed, keeping 78 acres as woodland and wetland, 22 acres in blueberry farm, and 20 acres as community vegetable garden plots leased to individuals growing for family tables. Large preserves are left strictly to wild creatures, no human entry.

At the south end is 75-acre Phantom Lake, elevation 250 feet, a designated "quiet zone," no motorboats, no loud radios, no whooping and hollering. Pond lilies bloom yellow on the waters (these are the native species, not the alien that blooms white on Lake Washington). Muskrats ramble through the willow swamps. Great blue heron fish. Bald eagles perch atop snags. A viewing platform permits a stroll out from shore to watch little birds chasing big birds away from nests.

The 1½ miles from Phantom Lake to Larsen Lake is the most popular natural-area walk in Bellevue. The way north is beside a working farm, 156 Avenue SE hedged off by shrubs. In ½ mile is a crossing of SE 16 Street to a parking lot by the ranger station; pick up guides to the wildlife, plants, and butterflies; ask about interpretive tours.

Muskrats ramble through the willow swamps. Great blue heron fish. Bald eagles perch atop snags. A viewing platform permits a stroll out from shore to watch little birds chasing big birds away from nests.

From the ranger station the trail leads between farms on the right, willow woods and cedar woods on the left. Signs explain the history, the ecology, and the habitats in forests and fields and sloughs of ospreys and red-tail hawks and kingfisher, river otter and coyote. In ½ mile the trail crosses Lake Hills Boulevard and passes the Lake Hills Library to a T.

The left goes ½ mile through woods and blueberry farm to 148 Avenue SE. The right proceeds by untamed marsh (a "wildlife enhancement area") and tamed blueberries to Larsen Lake. Frogs splash and ducks paddle and fish swim. A pier thrusts out through lily pads for views. Murky waters of Kelsey Creek are crossed. At ¾ mile from the T is 148 Avenue SE and a sidewalk that facilitates a loop.

WEOWNA PARK

Round trip: 1 mile
Maps: 6, 7

Directions: *Weowna Park is on the western shore of Lake Sammamish. From West Lake Sammamish Parkway SE, go west on SE 26 Street, then right on 168 Avenue SE. The park is on the left, with limited street parking on side streets to the right.*

Virgin forest, a strip 1 mile long and ¼ mile wide? Douglas fir up to 6 feet in diameter? In the heart of Bellevue? How come? A complicated tale; suffice to say here that "Weowna" does not come from the vocabulary of the Original Inhabitants but from the puffery of a developer who sold lots to purchasers who could say, "We own a park." So how come Douglas firs and no houses? Located on the "breaks" from Lake Hills to Lake Sammamish the ¼ mile width is unbuildable cliff.

Trees aside, the center of interest is Phantom Creek, which emerges from a culvert under 168 Avenue SE at SE 19 and slices a

Weowna Park

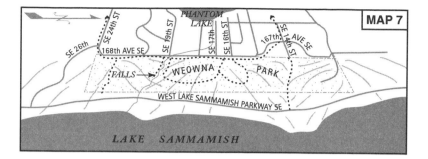

chasm in the cliff's glacial debris. To reveal a secret, the creek is not natural. It was dug to drain much of Phantom Lake to make dry pasture. Hard digging in the nineteenth century, through hardpan. In this twenty-first century, measures are being taken to keep the chasm from eating back and swallowing up the Shopping Square or a ballfield.

The wise plan is to walk from the top, 168th, elevation 275 feet. A walkway extends 1 mile along the park's upper edge. The lower edge is fenced off by houses; the one trail from West Lake Sammamish Parkway, elevation 100 feet, has no parking worth mentioning. From the top, paths lead down both sides of Phantom Creek to views of the chasm amid the big trees.

KIRKLAND WATERSHED PARK

Loop trip: 2 miles
High point: 400 feet
Elevation gain: 200 feet
Map: 8

How much good stuff can be crammed into 60 acres? The forest grown since turn-of-the-century logging—large Douglas fir, huge maples dripping licorice fern, groves of madrona, fine big cedars, alder, and hemlock, the occasional gigantic cottonwood, mysterious plantations of two-needle (lodgepole?) pine. Thickets of yellowberries, white lawns of candyflower. Canyons carved in glacial drift, creeks trickling through horsetail bottoms. Mysterious artifacts (named by David Quimby) of a vanished civilization (hypothesized by him). And sampling it all, a roundabout, up-and-down-and-up loop trail of some 2 miles.

Directions: *Go off I-405 on Exit 17 and turn west on NE 70 Place, which bends south as NE 68 Street. Turn south on 108 Avenue NE to a*

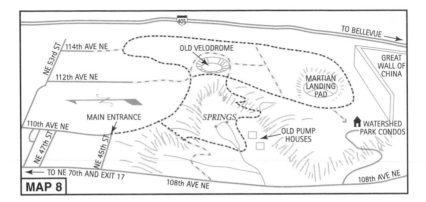

two-car parking space at the main park entrance, 110 Avenue NE at NE 45 Street. Elevation, 400 feet.

To do the loop in the recommended clockwise direction, set off up the main trail (old service road, abandoned). Pass a major trail descending to the right; this is the return leg. The path skirts the edge of a precipice plunging to a green canyon on the right and ascends to the plateau top at 425 feet. An entry trail from 112 Avenue NE joins on the left just before the first of the artifacts, the Old Velodrome.

For the loop, keep north through fine woods. But hark! What is that roar? One had forgotten there are freeways. The trail bends around to head south, passing an entry from 114 Avenue NE, and emerges from forest at the huge bowl, the Martian Landing Pad. What is that emptiness above, where formerly was a green roof? It is the sky! With swallows in it! Keep straight ahead to the Great Wall of China. Look out to towers of downtown Bellevue, to heights of the Issaquah Alps. Reenter forest, the canyon gaping on the left, and proceed north to a Y a few steps short of the Old Velodrome.

Now for the nicest part of the walk, though the trail is thin and steep and slippery. Take the left fork and switchback down the precipice, deeper and deeper into the green. Pause to rest on hillside benches. Look through the treetops, down to the birds, out to glimpses of Lake Washington. But what has happened to one's hearing? The roaring has stopped! When the ears dropped off the brink the freeway dematerialized, was shipped to Mars. Birdsongs submerge the generalized humrumble of the distant city.

Birdsongs submerge the generalized humrumble of the distant city.

At the bottom of the canyon

the springs seep out of aquifers, through horsetails, joining to form a creek. The path crosses, climbs to the narrow crest of a ridge to a **T**. The right climbs to complete the loop.

KIRKLAND WATERFRONT

One way: 5 miles
High point: 100 feet
Elevation gain: minor
Maps: 9A, 9B

Bellevue is the "city between the lakes." Kirkland, dating from an earlier time of fewer shoreline-hugging plutocrats, is the "city on the lake." The goal of its Parks Department is a continuous walkway beside or near the water the 5 miles from Juanita Bay to Yarrow Bay. Partly in open marsh, partly on beach, partly through lanes of marinas and condos and eateries and shops, it is such a route as cannot be matched. The imaginative way is to do the whole thing at a single go, loitering as lazily as may be wished, counting on the bus to whisk the bones back to the start.

Of all the walking routes described in these pages, this is the favorite of tourists. The views, yes. A jubilee of art galleries, bistros, antique shops, jazz joints, restaurants–latte shops–pizza parlors. On

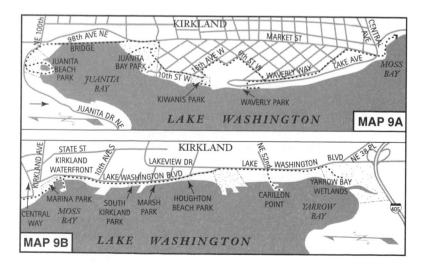

fine days, more naked flesh than can be seen elsewhere in the Northwest without a cover charge.

Directions: *The north end of the Kirkland Waterfront is anchored by Juanita Beach Park, on Juanita Drive NE. From I-405, take exit 18 (NE 85 Street/Kirkland) and go downhill toward the waterfront on NE 85 Street, which becomes Central Avenue. At a stop sign go right on Market Street, which eventually becomes 98 Avenue NE. Turn left at a stop sign on Juanita Drive NE. Go left into the park entrance at the next light, 97 Avenue NE.*

The next 2 miles are on quiet residential streets, side trips to parklets: Kiwanis (wild shore, huge cottonwoods); Waverly ("Skinnydipper").

The succeeding 2 miles, the Shoreline (ultimately) Trail, are where Kirkland has rings on its fingers, bells on its toes. When the decision was made to be "a lakeside town rather than a town near a lake," this was the first city in the state to complete—in 1974—a shoreline master program pursuant to the State Shoreline Management Act of 1971. It is the only city to envision a trail all the way along its portion of Lake Washington. Since 1973 it has required developers to provide public walkways across private property on the shore. Though the

Kirkland waterfront

walkway is interrupted by (temporary) dead ends, requiring detours via the sidewalk, the pedestrian is beside the lake most of the entire 2 miles from Marina Park to Yarrow Bay wetlands.

The start is Marina Park, built in 1970 exactly where Market Street used to run out to a ferry dock; until the end of War II a person could walk on the boat, debark in 4 miles at Madison Park, and catch the bus to downtown Seattle.

Beyond, broken only by shops and condos, a string of entertainments: Port of Moss Bay Marina (poor people can look at, but mustn't touch, toys of the rich people); Street End Park, a 0.2-acre window on the water; South Kirkland Park (another little look); Marsh Park ("Muscle Beach," the favorite stage for mating rituals); Houghton Beach (where families huddle under the lifeguard, defender of public morals).

Then Carillon Point, site until 1946 of the Lake Washington shipyard, which built ferries, War I wooden freighters, postwar steel freighters, and War II destroyer escorts. In 1989 the Skinner Corporation cut the ribbon for the grand opening of a 100-room hotel, a 461-slip marina, 150 apartments and condo units, 1746 parking stalls, all this plus shops galore on "31 acres along a breathtaking section of waterfront," becoming (said Skinner) "the pendant on the necklace of Kirkland waterfront parks."

Then Yarrow Bay wetlands, third-largest marsh (it was) on Lake Washington, battleground for a half-century over drying up and paving the wet or leaving it alone. In 1986 Kirkland caved in to "private property rights" and permitted The Plaza at Yarrow Bay. The philanthropic developer "gave" the city 66 acres of cattails, blackbirds, muskrats, and woodpeckers, defended from human entry by hardhack and willow-tangle and hellberries, bless them.

JUANITA BAY PARK

Round trip: 1½ miles
High point: 50 feet
Elevation gain: minor
Map: 9A

Directions: *Park along Juanita Drive in a lot where 98 Avenue NE rises from the swamps.*

This "largest jewel in Kirkland's tiara of waterfront parks" is also

In winter, as many as 1600 birds have been counted at a time: osprey, barn owls, bald eagles, herons, downy and hairy woodpeckers.

the city's largest park, 103-odd acres, 2100 feet of shoreline. It became possible when a golf course, converted from a French-run frog-legs farm in 1932, closed in 1975, and the citizenry voted funds to fend off a millionaires' row.

No bawfields here, no kinetics, no boatlaunch. Rather, "an alternative to our structured everyday lives." The Southern Meadow, upland, is mowed, irrigated, manicured, and provided with play area, picnic shelter, benches, and a paved trail through groves of weeping willow and birch, Douglas fir and maple. The Wetland Meadow is left for Nature to manage, supervised by bossy blackbirds. Two dead-end boardwalks permit dry-foot, non-destructive walking out through the buttercups and yellow flag and cattails to views of marsh and lake. The highest priority is wildlife habitat.

The abandonment of a stretch of highway converted a causeway built in 1935 into a path crossing ½ mile of bayshore and Forbes Creek wetlands. The structure was replaced in the 1990s by a new-built promenade bridge. Muskrat and raccoon and opossum and beaver and skunk live here, and more than seventy species of birds; in winter, as many as 1600 birds have been counted at a time: osprey, barn owls, bald eagles, herons, downy and hairy woodpeckers. Salmon spawn in Forbes Creek.

ST. EDWARD STATE PARK

Loop trips: 4½ miles
High point: 350 feet
Elevation gain: 338 feet
Map: 10

Directions: *Drive Juanita Drive NE north from Kirkland or south from Kenmore to the obscure park entrance at NE 145th. Turn west to a Y and keep right to the parking, elevation 350 feet.*

In 1977 Puget Sound City obtained—half a century after any realist would have judged the last chances long gone—a wildland park on Lake Washington. The necessary fortuities were: a property owner (the Archdiocese of Seattle) with soul, and an anomalously alert group of state and federal legislators and officials.

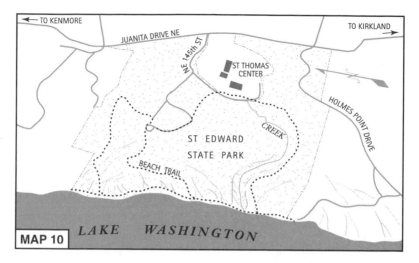

TO KENMORE

JUANITA DRIVE NE

TO KIRKLAND

NE 145th ST

ST THOMAS CENTER

HOLMES POINT DRIVE

CREEK

ST EDWARD STATE PARK

BEACH TRAIL

MAP 10 LAKE WASHINGTON

No raw wasteland was this, such as was obtained from the U.S. Navy the same year, at Sand Point, but instant wildland park, the forests already installed. Most of the 316 acres—all the steep bluff and the several superb ravines and the 3000 feet of waterfront—will remain as they were under stewardship of the Church—green and quiet.

Where to walk? Where the seminary students did for years and the deer and coyote still do, tramping out a trail system of a dozen-odd miles. For a sampler, do a figure-8 loop of some 4½ miles.

From the main building descend the Beach Trail, losing 338 feet in ⅔ mile, through a forest of maple, alder, dogwood, hazelnut, cedar, Douglas fir, and madrona. Views into shadowed vales give the feeling of touring the great halls of a forest mansion. Side trails invite left and right.

For the first loop follow the shore trail ¼ mile along the waterside terrace (underwater until the lake was lowered) to the south boundary. Retrace steps to the picnic lawns at the foot of the Beach Trail. Watch mallard hens convoy flotillas of ducklings, gaze to boats on the water, to Kenmore up the lake and Sand Point down. Then, just to the south, take a prominent path up a ravine to a skinny ridge crowned by a cathedral forest, and at ⅔ mile from the shore leave trees for lawns of the St. Thomas enclave and follow roads and grass paths north ½ mile to the start.

For the second loop, again descend the Beach Trail—or one of those mentally noted sidepaths. Turn north on the shore through a succession of monster cottonwoods, two with caves that invite kids to

St. Edward State Park

crawl in. In ½ mile the park ends. Retreat a few hundred steps to the only major uptrail. The way climbs steeply through glorious fir forest, then sidehills a jungle gorge where devil's club grows tall as trees. At the Y the left fork drops to the creek and climbs to suburbia; take the right a final bit up to the plateau and at ⅔ mile from the lake return to the parking lot.

REDMOND WATERSHED PARK

Round trip: 3 miles
High point: 525 feet
Elevation gain: minor
Map: 11

Between 1926 and 1944 Redmond bought 806 acres as a buffer to Seidel Creek, expected to supply domestic water. The creek never passed purity tests and the tract, which had been railroad-logged by the 1920s, was let alone to grow new trees—with the exception of a wide swath of nakedness through the middle for burial of a natural gas line. The 1986 master plan dedicated the forest to "low intensity" use, meaning the expulsion of the motorcycles that had conquered it. Where the public hypocrisy is manifested is in the definition of "low." Redmond hav-

Cedars self-sculpt themselves into graceful shrubs. Red huckleberry bushes top old stumps. Vine maple arches over trickle-creeks. The forest climaxes in a cathedral of maple and fir.

ing anointed itself as the Bicycle Capital of the Solar System, the city daddies and mommies have had to keep straight faces while declaring that muscle-powered (and gravity-powered) wheels going 10–20 miles per hour are much less intense than hydrocarbon-powered wheels. Even pedestrians who live close by won't find much peace here except on rainy Tuesday mornings in February. One trail, however, deserves regional attention, if only to give due warning.

Directions: *Drive Avondale Road from downtown Redmond. At a Y bear easterly on Novelty Hill Road 2 miles to just short of the Northwest Natural Gas pipeline swatch. Turn left to the parking area, elevation 525 feet.*

A nature trail fondles a tiny wetland. The main trail, an old logging road, sidehills a vale of Seidel Creek, burrowing through silvery alder, lacy hemlock, sprawling maple, and cottonwood that fluffs the spring air. Cedars self-sculpt themselves into graceful shrubs. Red huckleberry bushes top old stumps. Vine maple arches over trickle-creeks. The forest climaxes in a cathedral of maple and fir.

At 1½ miles the path drops to cross a sparkling tributary of Seidel Creek. The park doesn't get any better than this.

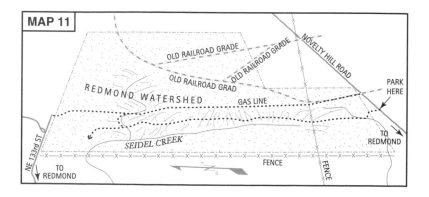

MAP 11
OLD RAILROAD GRADE
OLD RAILROAD GRADE
NOVELTY HILL ROAD
OLD RAILROAD GRAD
REDMOND WATERSHED
GAS LINE
PARK HERE
SEIDEL CREEK
NE 133rd ST
TO REDMOND
TO REDMOND
FENCE
FENCE

TOLT PIPELINE

One way: 12 miles
High point: 550 feet
Elevation gain: 1200 feet
Maps: 12A, 12B

When the Seattle Water Department built the pipeline to the city in 1963 from its new Tolt River Reservoir 30 miles away, it acquired for the purpose a strip of land some 100 feet wide. A great and famous victory it was for a new principle in sharing when King County Parks was granted rights to use a 12-mile stretch of the pipeline corridor for feet, horses, and bicycles, up hill and down dale, from city's edge through suburbia to the Snoqualmie River valley.

Not to belittle the pioneering achievement, the Tolt "trail" (a service road for trucks) has lost most of its old popularity among pedestrians. Walking the entire 12 miles (times two) in 1977, I was exhilarated by the progression from urban to suburban to exurban to lonesome, the progressive nearing of the Cascades from each hill topped,

Fog-filled Snoqualmie Valley from the Tolt Pipeline

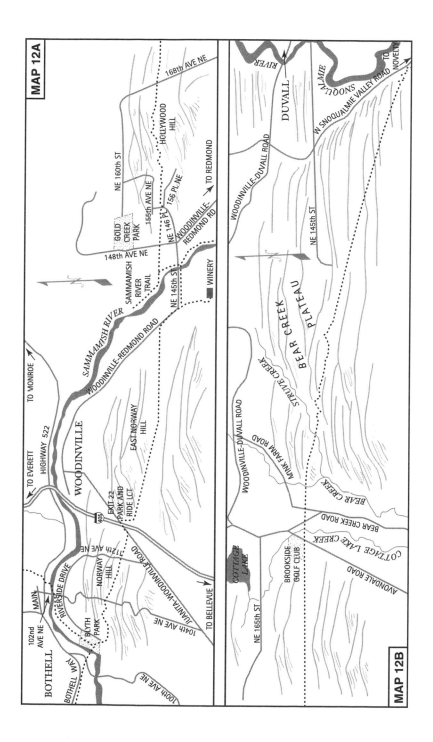

168th AVE NE

HOLLYWOOD HILL

NE 160th ST

TO REDMOND

155th AVE NE

156 PL NE

NE 146 PL

WOODINVILLE-REDMOND RD

GOLD CREEK PARK

148th AVE NE

SAMMAMISH RIVER TRAIL

SAMMAMISH RIVER

NE 145th ST

WINERY

WOODINVILLE-REDMOND ROAD

TO MONROE

TO EVERETT

HIGHWAY 522

WOODINVILLE

EAST NORWAY HILL

EXIT 23 PARK AND RIDE LOT

I 405

12th AVE NE

NORWAY HILL

JUANITA-WOODINVILLE ROAD

104th AVE NE

TO BELLEVUE

RIVERSIDE DRIVE

MAIN

102nd AVE NE

BLYTH PARK

BOTHELL

BOTHELL WAY

100th AVE NE

DUVALL

SNOQUALMIE RIVER

TO NOVELTY

W SNOQUALMIE VALLEY ROAD

WOODINVILLE-DUVALL ROAD

NE 145th ST

BEAR CREEK PLATEAU

STRUVE CREEK

WOODINVILLE-DUVALL ROAD

MINK FARM ROAD

BEAR CREEK

BEAR CREEK ROAD

COTTAGE LAKE CREEK

AVONDALE ROAD

COTTAGE LAKE

BROOKSIDE GOLF CLUB

NE 165th ST

the wide wet green of intervening valleys—and the compression of all this varied experience in a single good long walk. That satisfaction is still available to any disciple of the good long walk. The variety of experience is, of course, different. More city every passing year. Less of the other.

Most of the walking nowadays is by bits and pieces, and mainly by people living close by. A half-dozen accesses to the "trail" from handy parking can break the 12 miles into bite size. The map in these pages, combined with a highway map, will guide the car.

Norway Hill to I-405, 1 mile, elevation gain 50 feet

I-405 to Sammamish River, scant 2 miles, elevation gain 125 feet

Sammamish River to Bear Creek valley, 4 miles, elevation gain 650 feet

Bear Creek Valley to Snoqualmie Valley, 4 miles, elevation gain 350 feet

Now, to whisper a secret known to few except the readers of my out-of-print *Footsore 2* and *Hiking the Mountains to Sound Greenway*: The best of the Tolt "trail" lies beyond. From Novelty (that is, the southern outskirts of Duvall), a gated (walk-by) service road climbs from the Snoqualmie Valley to, first, scattered stumpranches, and then the empty opens of a tree farm that extends to the upthrusting scarp of the Cascades. Though not "official," the walking is freely open to the Tolt Forks that were the favorite destination of my Troop 324 (and a whole lot of other troops), to the awesome canyon of the North Fork, where the river is deeper than it is wide, and to the gate that bars entry to the watershed.

SAMMAMISH RIVER ONCE AND FUTURE TRAIL

One way: 10 miles
High point: 50 feet
Elevation gain: none
Maps: 13A, 13B

In 1977, before the Save the Sammamish Trail Association won its famous victory, I walked the 10 miles from Redmond to Bothell, and the 10 miles back from Bothell to Redmond, and in all the long day met nobody but cows drugged out on cuds and lonesome horses wanting a hug. Murky waters floated ducks and coots. Tweetybirds flitted in reeds, clouds of gulls circled, hawks patrolled. Pastures

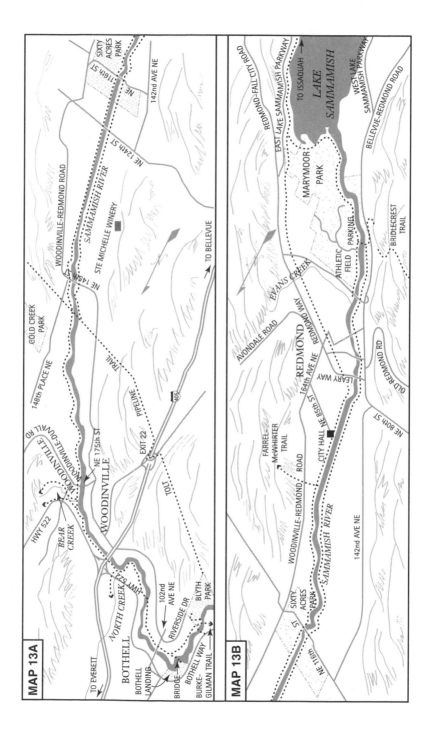

and cornfields sprawled table-flat east and west to forested valley wall, muting the faraway highways. Accustomed to skulking dark woods, I was dizzied by the size of the sky.

On a fine spring Sunday of 1981 I found the new-built trail united in one big smile. Bicycles by the family (rentals in Bothell and Redmond), rollerskaters by the platoon, horses rejoicing in the companionship of riders, joggers, walkers, and, on the parallel water trail, kayaks and canoes and rubber rafts. Tiny children were staggering-toddling or being carried on parents' backs, in the kiddyseats on bikes, in strollers pushed by fathers on rollerskates. The age-challenged were enjoying the sunshine on a flat, paved, no-obstacle path (beside it, a gravel horse path). Everyone yielded to wheelchairs. It was a scene to start tears of joy, to prove the innate goodness of humanity, the providence of the "multi-use trail."

Nor was this the last of the good news. Since 1989, more than 700 volunteers of the Friends of the Sammamish River have been revegetating the riverbanks, and in 1994 King County Parks joined in. The King County Farmlands Preservation Program was funded by the voters and through 1985 had bought development rights to 70 percent of the valley's agricultural lands, nearly 1000 acres in total.

There seemed no end of good. King County Parks consolidated ownership and easements along the west bank of the river for a second and parallel trail. A campaign was making headway to undo some of the evil wreaked by the farmers who in the 1930s–1940s channelized the river to claim nature's wetness for man's croplands, the holocaust completed by the U.S. Army Corps of Engineers in 1965, when it shortened up the meanders, cleaned out shore jungles and slough swamps, mowed the banks to prevent an infestation of nesting birds and rambling muskrats, and made 30 miles of wildlife habitat into 14 miles of ditch.

So why am I not smiling anymore? Why am I muttering, ". . . rainy Tuesday morning in February?" Wheels. The same thing is happening here as on the Burke-Gilman. "Walkers of the world unite! Take up your quarterstaffs and give the blithering bikers the what for!"

Really, now, there would have been no need for World War II had Europe imprisoned Hitler in 1932 for terminal silliness. When King County Parks gets off its pension-protecting bottom and installs barrier-enforced separation between lanes for (1) bikers-skaters-runners and (2) walkers and wheelchair-users and baby-strollers, there can be once more, and forevermore, the joy I found that fine spring Sunday of 1981.

Directions: *From Main Street in Bothell drive the 102 Avenue* *bridge over the river and turn right on Riverside Drive to Blyth Park, elevation 25 feet.*

Blyth Park, Bothell's biggest at 36 acres, is the junction of the Burke-Gilman and Sammamish River Trails-That-Were and the Tolt Pipeline. The trail turns upstream, through cottonwood-alder-willow forest, beside cattails and reeds raucous with blackbirds. At ½ mile from Blyth Park is The Park at Bothell Landing.

When Bothell turned its back on its beginnings as a stop for the steamers coming up from Lake Washington and—in high enough water—proceeding to Lake Sammamish, it became just another hick village selling gas and groceries and the occasional hamburger. Briefly, after 1912, it could boast of lying on the Pacific Highway from Seattle to Everett. However, this soon became "the old Everett Highway" and the hamlet moldered. When it once again turned its face to the river it got Soul. The shops on the mall of Bothell Landing offer ice cream cones, books, and tee shirts. The Park at Bothell Landing is a dandy spot to watch ducks and canoes, to picnic, to swim. Of historic interest are the buildings: the 1885 Beckstrom Log House; the 1896 Lytle House, now the Senior Center; and the 1893 William Hannan Home, now the Bothell Historical Museum (Sundays, 1:00 P.M.–4:00 P.M.).

Landing Park, elevation 20 feet, lies just off Bothell Way, and ¼ mile from its graceful wooden bridge arching over the river is 102 Avenue NE. At ¾ mile from the bridge (1¼ miles from Blyth), the trail crosses the river to another popular parking-starting place just off Highway 522. For a short bit the way is a sidewalk along the old Bothell–Woodinville Road, which now dead-ends at the river. A bridge over North Creek leads to a forest of concrete pillars whose foliage is concrete ramps—the interchanges of I-405 and Highway 522 and whatnot.

At 2¾ miles from Blyth Park the trail crosses Bear Creek and goes under NE 175 Street in Woodinville (parking). The scene changes. To this point there have been river and greenery but also trailer courts, apartment houses, assorted urbia, and concrete. Now begins ruralia as the broad trail and companion river strike out into the center of the plain. At 4¼ miles is the junction with the Tolt Pipeline and at 4¾ miles the underpass crossing of NE 145 Street (parking and sidetrip to Ste. Michelle Winery, ¼ mile away, to buy cheese and crackers for lunch—the winery has 90 manicured acres for strolling). Directly across the street is the Redhook Brewery and Pub, for those with less highbrow tastes.

Shortly beyond the underpass crossing of NE 124 Street (parking), at 7¼ miles is NE 116 Street and the county's Sixty Acres Park—stay out unless you're wearing team togs and kicking a soccer ball. At 8 miles is the junction with Redmond's Farrel-McWhirter Trail.

At 8½ miles the scene again changes at Redmond City Hall, beside the river the dead end of NE 85 Street (parking). Watch for the Levine sculpture, *Sitting Woman*, who is doing it without a chair.

The trail follows the river from farms through city, passing under lofty masses of highway concrete, and at 8¾ miles crosses Leary Way next to "downtown" Redmond. Across the river is where the Public Trust (abandoned golf course needed for park) was vanquished by Private Greed (yet another shopping mall). At 10 miles from Blyth Park is the entrance to Marymoor Park.

Here, the Public Trust won, and what began in 1904 as the Clise Family hunting preserve and became a dairy farm was purchased in 1963 by King County for a 485-acre park, bawfields, tennis courts, archery butts, model airplane airport, bicycle tracks, picnic tables, teeter totters and swings, Pea Patch. An exhibit of the dig that confirmed human residence on this spot 7000 years ago. A river. A lake.

Not a whole lot of walking, though not to be disdained is simply roaming through the fields under the big sky. The best stroll is downstream along the riverbank, from fields and Pea Patch and willow thickets to marshes and, finally, a wooden walkway to a concrete viewing pier at the meeting of reeds and open lake, by the beginning of the Sammamish River, in views down the 9 miles of lake to Tiger Mountain, rising 3000 feet above the south end.

The Bridlecrest Trail climbs 2 miles through forest, then backyards and fenced pastures, to Bridle Trails State Park, giving horses an off-road connection to the Sammamish River Trail.

A link across the southeastern section of Marymoor hooks the Sammamish River Trail to the Lake Sammamish Trail.

LAKE SAMMAMISH TRAIL

One way: 11 miles
High point: 100 feet
Elevation gain: none
Map: 14

'Twas on a fine Sunday in 1979 or so that the Cascade Bicycle Club, largest in the nation, and my Issaquah Alps Trails Club, one of the

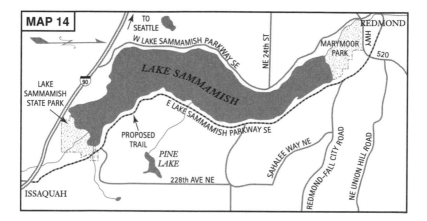

feistiest, staged a joint march from Issaquah to Redmond on the rail-road beside Lake Sammamish. Well, no, not many of us were actually on, what with surly millionaires and their brandished shotguns and chained mastiffs threatening to loose the jaws and pull the triggers if we "trespassed" on the public property they sought to privatize.

In 1980 Burlington Northern confirmed plans to go away. Cheered on by the citizenry that had won the Burke-Gilman and the Sammamish River, King County Parks began drawing plans for an 11-mile trail. Our local millionaires poured some of their millions into the national campaign dedicated to defeating the Rails-to-Trails program adopted by Congress.

Much as I used to enjoy peaceful strolls by docks and boats, wild-tangled swamp greenery, sun-sparkling waves, sailboats, and the panorama from the Squak Plain to summits of the Issaquah Alps, for some years I've left the battleground to the lawyers and attack dogs and shotguns.

The public's kingdom will come, its will be done, on the trail. So much for Sammamish War I. Then will begin War II, between we once (and future!) allies. I plan to pretty much sit that one out. Sooner or later King County Parks will face up to the fact you can't dump all the pussycats in the same gunnysack and hope they'll all come out alive.

OTHER TRIPS

Pioneer Park. A deep green ravine, a year-round stream, the wild gem of the City of Mercer Island. No golf course, not yet.

Farrel-McWhirter Park and Trail. The 200-acre pasture and forest, formerly a working farm, has been hailed as "the jewel of Redmond's park system." The 2 miles of in-park trails and the 3-mile

600-year-old Douglas fir in O. O. Park

trail to the Sammamish River Trail are the heart of the north King County horse country.

O. O. Denny–Big Finn Hill Park. From a ¼-mile strip of Lake Washington public beach a path ascends Big Finn Creek to the snag of a Douglas fir that was nigh onto 600 years old when the top blew out in a big wind. Was 26.3 feet, in circumference. And still is.

MacDonald (Tolt River) Park. Riverbank and valley-wall trails at the confluence of the Tolt and Snoqualmie Rivers, on a site of a major village of the Original Inhabitants.

Hazel Wolf Wetlands Preserve. One of the very few lonely places on the plateau, at the headwaters of Laughing Jacobs Creek, 116 acres of watery wildlife refuge. Established by the Land Conservancy and King County adjoining Plateau Golf Course. The Main Trail (foot and horse) and Ann's (Weinmann) Footpath total 1 mile. Trailhead is a cul de sac at the end of SE Windsor Boulevard.

Opposite: *Mount Rainier from Middle Tiger Mountain*

ISSAQUAH ALPS

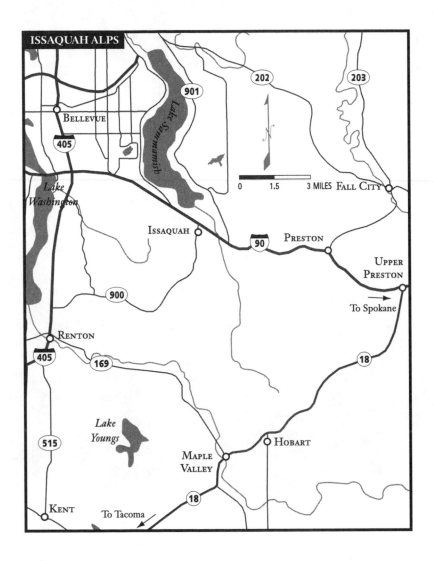

ISSAQUAH ALPS

Management: King County Parks, Washington State Parks, State Department of Natural Resources, Issaquah Parks Department
Topographic maps: USGS Mercer Island, Issaquah, Maple Valley, Hobart, Fall City, Snoqualmie—and their equivalents in the Green Trails series, privately published. Issaquah Alps Trails Club maps: Cougar Mountain, Squak Mountain, Tiger Mountain

An expanse of 20,000-odd acres along Interstate 90 between Seattle and the Cascade front constitutes the largest urban wildland (not merely *near* but totally *within* "Puget Sound City") in America.

Elevations range from near sea level at Lake Washington to 3500 feet. The 200-plus miles of foot trails provide most of the wheelfree wildland walking a half-hour from homes in King Country and three adjoining counties.

Trails range from flat to moderate to steep. They are readily walkable the year around, though at times the highest reaches offer easy (no treacherous footgear required) ventures into winter, the snowball-throwing country.

Many a night, while a student at the University of Washington, I clambered to the roof of Parrington Hall and wondered at the blinking lights strung in a line eastward into darkness, the beacons guiding Sons of Lindy through the Cascades. Whenever the press has occasion to notice the existence of the heights nearest Seattle, lifting literally from the shore of Lake Washington to the elevation of Snoqualmie Pass, they are usually described as "foothills of the Cascades." My position on the matter is that Seattle is built on seven foothills of the Issaquah Alps.

Granted the name is new, dating only from 1976. Moreover, certain editorial powers in the press are intimately hitched to Interests that are all too aware I devised the name to give the peaks a politically useful unity, a focus for efforts to preserve the "wildness within" Puget Sound City (which the late Emmett Watson strenuously argued was not at all the same thing as the "Greater Seattle" touted by the Interests).

The Issaquah Alps Trails Club, founded in 1979, is distrusted by the lord high executors of the Private Greed Doctrine because its allegiance is to the Public Trust Doctrine. These two philosophies of

91

government contended during the framing of the United States Constitution, as they had during the confrontation at Runnymede, and are still at it, nowhere more vigorously than east of Lake Washington.

COUGAR MOUNTAIN REGIONAL WILDLAND PARK
Maps: 15, 16, 17

In 1980 the Trails Club publicly proposed that King County establish a "great big green and quiet place" on Cougar Mountain, centered on its highest summit, 1595 feet, and the valley of Coal Creek draining to Lake Washington. In 1985 King County Executive Randy Revelle held a press conference atop Anti-Aircraft Peak to formally dedicate the park. In 1994 the King County Council adopted a master plan for the 3000 acres the park by then encompassed, and by ordinance dedicated it to *low-impact, nonmechanized* recreation.

That tumultuous time was made the more so by the advent of the fat-tire bike and the well-financed campaign by the new industry to

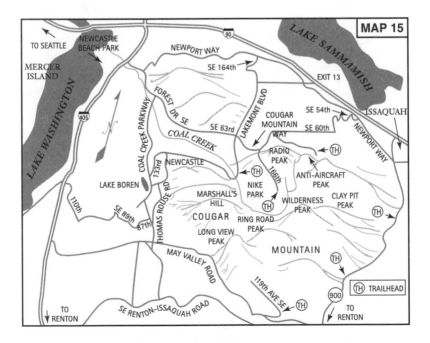

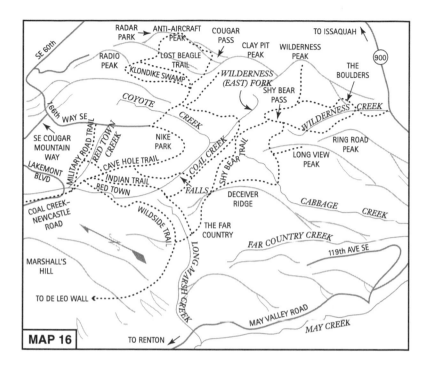

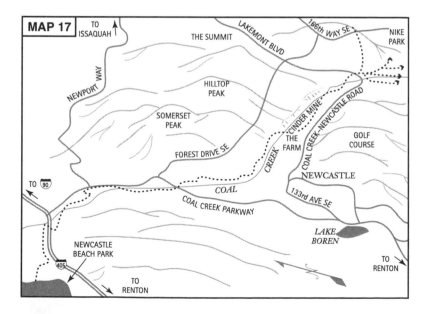

"conquer" (as its spokespeople boasted they would do) Cougar. The reader is referred to the history I wrote ("How We Got the Park") as introduction to the 2000 edition of the trail guide to Cougar Mountain, published by the club, written by Charles McCrone.

Because the book exists and is sold at every book and boot shop that knows its business, in these pages I confined myself to an introductory sampling.

COAL CREEK TOWNSITE

Loop trip: 1 mile
High point: 500 feet
Elevation gain: 100 feet
Maps: 15, 16

Newcastle—the original, not to be confused with the mini-Bellevue incorporated in the 1990s—was a floating sort of town. The initial main settlement, "Old Newcastle" or "Old Town," was at a site now lying off the Coal Creek–Newcastle Road on 72nd. The final center was the town of Coal Creek, or "New Town," referred to here as Coal Creek Townsite.

In the middle of where the town used to be is today's Red Town Trailhead, the most popular entry to the park, the start of trails reaching to every far corner. However, the favorite is right here, on a looping mile so easy it can be done in a quick half-hour, so rich in history it can fill a fascinating half-day.

Directions: *Go off I-90 on Exit 13, ascend Lakemont Boulevard over "The Pass," and go down to cross Coal Creek. At the sharp bend of the crossing a side road leads to the trailhead, elevation 600 feet.*

A new visitor's first reaction, trying to see beneath the half-century of greening to the decades of industrial grime, of human work and play, happiness and tragedy, is to ask, "Where did the town all go?" The guidebook of the Trails Club tells much of the story. The all of it is in another book published by the club, *Coals of Newcastle*, by Lucile and Dick McDonald.

As a prelude to the loop, take the short path into the gulch of Red Town Creek. Pass the Military Road (trail, now), which went over the mountain and down to Issaquah. Spot in the creek an exposure of the No. 4 Seam; at an exposure like this, downstream, the riches of Coal Creek were discovered in 1863.

Mine shaft near Newcastle railroad terminus

Then, from the parking area walk straight ahead on the flat of the Wildside Trail. The path follows the grade of a road once used to haul logs to a sawmill and, after that, by the gypo miners who took over the area when the Pacific Coast Coal Company quit in 1930. The Bagley Seam lies beneath the trail as it passes the Bagley Seam Trail, climbing left, and crosses Coal Creek at the site of the Wash House, whose foundations lie buried under a heap of waste rock dumped by the gypos. The company miners coming off shift went directly to the Wash House and then home, where they were cleaner than their wives—who in the era of suffragette agitation eventually were granted a weekly Ladies Day. The way intersects the Rainbow Town Trail. Turn left on it to the concrete arch of the Ford Slope, which from 1910 to 1926 was the center of company mining, embodying the newest technology. It went down the Muldoon Seam at a 42-degree angle for 1740 feet (850 vertical feet, to 250 feet below sea level). Eleven electric locomotives worked underground on a number of levels in the Muldoon and adjoining seams. The coal was lifted to the surface by a steam hoist, the mine cars hauled down Coal Creek by the electrics for dumping in the top of the bunkers, which loaded rail cars for transport to Seattle.

Continue on the road-trail uphill from the Ford Slope, passing a side trail, right, to a concrete dam in Coal Creek that was almost completely buried by gravels of a 1990s flood. The reservoir (that was) supplied water to the mining operation and doubled as a sawmill pond. It tripled as the ol' swimmin' hole, where on alternate days in summer the girls swam and boys hid out in the woods, and the boys swam and girls hid out, swimming garb of the time being strictly that issued by Mother Nature.

The road climbs to a T, 750 feet, with the Indian Trail (here called Red Town Trail), used by the Original Inhabitants for overland travel between Coal Creek and May Creek, and later by farmers and miners. Turn left through Red Town, a principal neighborhood of Coal Creek, eighty houses on four streets. The name (invented and mainly used by children) came from the color the houses were painted by the company, which owned them. Other neighborhoods were White Town, Rainbow Town, Finn Town, and Greek Village. The trail crosses the 1000-foot-wide band in which the coal seams of the Newcastle Anticline intersect the surface: from south to north, the Jones, Dolly Varden, Ragtime, Shoo Fly, Muldoon, May Creek, Bagley, No. 3, and No. 4; off by itself to the north, dating from a later geological age, is the Primrose Seam.

Pass a sidepath left, the Bagley Seam Trail, descending a ravine formed by the collapse of an entry tunnel; the Cave Hole Trail right; and the site, on the right, of the palatial Superintendent's House. Turn left and descend Hill Street to the Red Town trailhead, passing the sites of the Hospital, the Doctor's House, and the Saloon.

RED TOWN BALLFIELD MEADOW PROJECT

Round trip: 1½ miles
High point: 650 feet
Elevation gain: 50 feet
Maps: 15, 16

The only spot near Red Town large enough and flat enough for baseball was the alluvial fan pushed out by Coal Creek into swamps of the old glacier trough, so that's where the town team in the Coal Country League, and later the local youth, played baseball.

The creation of the wildland park stirred Penny Manning to think how fitting it would be to have a showcase there for native plants of the western Washington meadows that had been obliterated by civilization. Though long abandoned and ravaged by time, the ballfield was still considerably meadowlike, or at least not forested. Thus in 1995 began the Project. King County Parks and the Issaquah Alps Trails Club were the sponsors. County and state agencies and private grants put up some money. Hundreds of volunteers put up a lot of muscle. The site was cleared of hellberry and scotchbroom and other "invasive exotics" (weeds) and topsoil was brought in. Native prairie/meadow bunchgrass, forbs, and riparian species have been planted (seventy-seven species) and native trees and shrubs (twenty-one species), a total of 6500 plants.

Come in late-May/June to see the bloom of camas, nodding onion, chocolate lily, Easter lily, and iris; June/August for lupine, penstemon, Erigeron, stonecrop, blue-eyed Mary, balsamroot; and August/September for the glorious straw-yellow extravaganza of the tall grasses. These are merely a few of the stars.

Directions: *Go off I-90 on Exit 13, ascend Lakemont Boulevard over "The Pass," and go down to cross Coal Creek. At the sharp bend of the crossing a side road leads to the Coal Creek Townsite trailhead, elevation 600 feet. Get there via the Red Town–Indian Trail or the Wildside Trail (see previous hike description). Or via loop. Sit*

> *Come in late-May/June to see the bloom of camas, nodding onion, chocolate lily, Easter lily, and iris; June/August for lupine, penstemon, Erigeron, stonecrop, blue-eyed Mary, balsamroot; and August/September for the glorious straw-yellow extravaganza of the tall grasses.*

on the benches (the park's only) and gaze. Until it goes dry in summer, listen to Coal Creek.

The Project is ongoing because the lamb of a meadow is surrounded and menaced by those bad old Eurasian weeds and the arrogant Washington forest (lions and tigers and bears). Should you wish to join the gardener/defender corps, the Washington Native Plants Society is the continuing sponsor. For information, send an email to *Aweinm@aol.com*, *ShannonB@pikemed.com*, or *pmanning@uswest.com*.

SEATTLE & WALLA WALLA RAILROAD

Round trip: to The Farm 3 miles, to Coal Creek Parkway 6 miles
Elevation loss: 170 feet to The Farm, 470 feet to the Parkway
Maps: 15, 16

Seattle's first railroad never got to Walla Walla but in 1878 did reach a profitable dead end at the Newcastle mines, then King County's major industry. In 1933, with the "company mine" already three years defunct, and only a few gypos still working underground and hauling their coal away in trucks, the railroad gave up the ghost. The town that once had rivaled Seattle as the county's largest was depopulated, rotting in the green, remnants being salvaged and scavenged and recycled, as was America's way on the frontier and during the Great Depression.

As far as The Farm the rail grade followed Coal Creek, incised in a wild green gorge downstream from Coal Creek Townsite, by the Forward Thrust bond issue of 1968 acquired for a county park. From The Farm the railroad struck off overland to Renton; local residents and Boy Scouts pioneered a rude path down the gorge. After creation of Cougar Mountain Regional Wildland Park, the contiguous Coal Creek Park began to receive attention.

The path is well tended (now) and easy, losing 170 feet of elevation from the Red Town trailhead to The Farm, and another 300 feet to Coal Creek Parkway.

What with residential "infilling" and thus all the new neighbors, the trailhead where Coal Creek Parkway takes a deep dip to cross the creek has become the most-used entry, but being stubborn I here will describe it from the Red Town trailhead, elevation 600 feet.

Directions: *Go off I-90 on Exit 13, ascend Lakemont Boulevard over*

Coal Creek Tributary

"The Pass," and go down to cross Coal Creek. At the sharp bend of the crossing a side road leads to the Coal Creek Townsite trailhead, elevation 600 feet. See previous hike description to Red Town trailhead.

Cross the county road to a field, pass a remnant of concrete foundation from the hotel, and at the field edge find the Coal Creek Trail (Elizabeth's Trail), descending the ravine dug for a tram which brought supplies up from the railroad to the hotel and company store. The path passes the awesome hole of an airshaft for a mine abandoned in 1886 and then splits. The left fork crosses the creek on a pretty bridge to the old rail grade, the route wide and level except for a detour around a slope of waste rock dumped from the gypo mines. Another pretty bridge recrosses the creek to unite the two forks. The united way soon comes to a third bridge, back across the creek to the rail grade.

The energy expenditure for the round trip is not great, but don't expect to do it in an easy hour. There's too much to muse on. Innumerable spur paths give delightful looks down to the creek as it steadily incises into the deep gorge. Benches allow comfortable admirations of the falls of the north fork of Coal Creek; above here the main fork goes dry in summer, the water seeping into the mines.

The informed and perceptive walker will spot bits and pieces of the past and conjure up that half-century bustle of railroading and mining: chunks of coal, brick, rusty iron; concrete foundations of a power plant and of the locomotive turntable; climbing roses blooming high in trees, the gaiety of apple-blossom time. Sites are passed of the railroad ticket office–waiting room and the coal bunkers, the takeoff of the spur line of the Washington Lumber and Spar logging railroad, which from 1920 to 1925 extended 13 miles of lines through the high basins. A side trail climbs from the valley to the site of the Newcastle School (1914–1969).

The history is near—submerged in the "new wilderness" rebuilt by nature in the past half-century; the tall, steep walls and lush forest of the gorge block out sights of civilization and soak up the noise, making room for the babble of creek and chirping of birds. In season, spawning salmon are fed upon by bald eagles, great blue heron, kingfishers, bears, coyotes, raccoons, and weasels; Coal Creek serves as a major link in the wildlife travel corridor between Lake Washington and the Cascades.

At a long 1 mile the grade is obliterated by the Cinder Mine, where waste rock dumped from the company mines was cooked by the spontaneous combustion of coal into pink and yellow clinkers. Until 1984 these were mined for processing into cinder blocks and running tracks. Beyond the pit the grade resumes and at a scant 1½ miles from the trailhead enters The Farm, as it was until 1977. Roaming the fields where the cows

In season, spawning salmon are fed upon by bald eagles, great blue heron, kingfishers, bears, coyotes, raccoons, and weasels; Coal Creek serves as a major link in the wildlife travel corridor between Lake Washington and the Cascades.

so recently grazed adds a pastoral element to the historical picture.

Shortly before The Farm, the Primrose Trail takes off from the rail grade down an old farm lane and passes an artificial pond (cattails, frogs, ducks) and a petite Grand Canyon where the creek cuts a wall of tawny sandstone and tumbles over tawny blocks ("Sandstone Falls"). The tributary Scalzo Creek enters, flowing from Tony Scalzo's mine in the Primrose Seam. In ¾ mile from the rail grade is a resumption of Coal Creek Trail, which in a scant 1 mile reaches Coal Creek Parkway.

COAL CREEK FALLS

Round trip: 2½ miles
High point: 950 feet
Elevation gain: 350 feet
Maps: 15, 16

Wetness is where the wildness mostly is, and if it splashes, the more festive the day's walk. That's why these falls are as popular a trip as the park has to offer.

Directions: *Go off I-90 on Exit 13, ascend Lakemont Boulevard over "The Pass," and go down to cross Coal Creek. At the sharp bend of the crossing a side road leads to the Coal Creek Townsite trailhead, elevation 600 feet.*

From Coal Creek Townsite trailhead, turn left up Hill Street, which on the flat of Red Town, 750 feet, bends right as the Red Town Trail, prelude to the Indian Trail. Just past the site of the Superintendent's House turn left, uphill, on Cave Hole Trail. Until establishment of the Regional Park, this route was driven by trucks of firewood loggers; earlier in the century, it was the horse-and-wagon access to the Klondike Reservoir and various coal prospects. The Pacific Coast Coal Company, builder of the road, took care not to undermine it by digging too close to the surface, but the latter-day gypos mined to the grass roots, causing the subsequent slumps of the ground surface known as "cave holes." The trail ascends to Clay Pit Road at 1200 feet, 1½ miles from the Coal Creek Townsite trailhead.

The ascent from Red Town zigs left across an open-pit mine in the No. 3 Seam and zags right to recross the No. 3, then the Bagley Seam; at the zag corner, a side trail goes off left to Red Town Creek dam and Military Road. At ⅔ mile, 950 feet, the Coal Creek Falls Trail goes right off the Cave Hole Trail. The way crosses the Bagley and Muldoon Seams, contours along slopes high above the Curious Valley, passes the

Coal Creek Falls Connector dropping to the Indian Trail, and turns a sharp left into the cleft of Coal Creek, and to the falls, 950 feet.

In winter the falls often thunder, boiling up gales of spray to fill the gorge. But often they fall dead silent, a crystal palace of icicles. In summer they also are quiet, a drip-drip-drip down the 30-foot slab, enough on the hottest of days to cool the shadows under the big hemlocks and maples. Granite erratics dropped by the glacier litter the potholes swirled out in the tawny bedrock sandstone. Coal Creek here is flowing over sedimentary structures; a stone's throw to the south the bedrock is volcanic, an andesite breccia.

Coal Creek

DE LEO WALL

Round trip: 4 miles
High point: 950 feet
Elevation gain: 350 feet
Maps: 15, 16

The De Leo family homesteaded at the base of 1125-foot Marshall's Hill a century and more ago. The steep slopes rising from May Valley culminate in a super-steepness several hundred feet tall. Views are over pastures and houses of May Valley to highlands concealing the Cedar River, to the eminence of Echo Mountain, and, most eminent of all, Rainier, and over the Big Valley of Renton-Southcenter-Kent-Auburn to the Sea-Tac Airport, the pulp mill plume of Tacoma, and where St. Helens used to be.

Directions: *Go off I-90 on Exit 13, ascend Lakemont Boulevard over "The Pass," and go down to cross Coal Creek. At the sharp bend of the crossing a side road leads to the Coal Creek Townsite trailhead, elevation 600 feet.*

From the Coal Creek Townsite trailhead, walk straight ahead on the Wildside Trail, over Coal Creek, past the Wash House site, and across the Rainbow Town Trail to a split. The right fork is the main Wildside way, but for a splendid short side loop take the left, the Steam Hoist Trail, to the massive concrete footings from whose anchoring a 2000-foot-long cable lifted five loaded mine cars at a time from depths of the Ford Slope. At a second split the right climbs from the valley floor to join the main-way Wildside. (But before doing that, take the left to the Millpond Dam, where a conduit built in 1916 carried Coal Creek 885 feet from the ol' swimmin' hole underneath the mineyards.)

The Curious Valley, trenched by a stream from the glacier front and vastly oversized for the amount of modern water, is shown on the maps as akin to Paul Bunyan's Round River in that it drains both ways at once, which is Curious indeed. The north end of the wetland, up to ⅛ mile wide, occupied by the impenetrable tulgeywood of the Long Marsh (actually, mostly Swamp, a little bit bog), empties to Coal Creek, the south end over Far Country Falls and down to May Creek. Along the east side of the valley runs the Red Town Trail, which on the way to the Far Country changes name to the Indian Trail.

The Wildside goes up a little, down a little, sidehill a lot, at 700 feet changing name to De Leo Wall Trail. The maples become majestic because the firewood cutters of the 1980s never got this far, and

De Leo Wall

the alders and cottonwood are bigger because the pulpwood loggers of the 1970s also quit, and the firs because no lumber-loggers have been here since the Coal Creek mill closed up shop in the 1920s.

Rounding a spur of Marshall's Hill, the way enters the haunting glen of Dave's Creek, a cold trickle in lushly moist shadows. What is that sound? Silence! The buzz of bees can be heard! Until a few more steps bring in earshot the never-ceasing, region-pervading rumble-drone of Sea-Tac Airport.

What is that sound? Silence! The buzz of bees can be heard!

At 950 feet are the promised views, from a buttress of andesite plucked steep by that old glacier. The grassy bald is edged by madrona, serviceberry, *Ceanothus sanguineus,* and Oregon white oak. If lucky *(not)* you may find poison oak. In spring the lunchroom is brightened by paintbrush and blue-eyed Mary and strawberry, honeysuckle and vetch and baldhip rose, Easter lily and chocolate lily, a garden growing to one side of the sky.

ANTI-AIRCRAFT PEAK TO CLAY PIT PEAK

Loop trip: 5½ miles
High point: 1525 feet
Elevation gain: 500 feet
Maps: 15, 16

Here is the sky country of Cougar Mountain, the high basins where Coal Creek pulls itself together from the seepages of Klondike Swamp, Coyote Swamp, and the East Fork, and where—across the low divide of Cougar Pass—West Fork Tibbetts Creek has its source in Lame Bear Swamp. This is wind country, where living gales roar through the trees, and cloud country, where storm-driven mists extinguish exterior reality. Finally, it's snow country, often white for weeks at a time and subject to blizzarding from October through April. Above the basins, ringing them to exclude too-vivid reminders of Puget Sound City, are three of Cougar's summits.

The trailhead of choice for quick views and a quick visit to winter is Radar Park, atop Anti-Aircraft Peak, where the Army had command radar for the Nikes.

Directions: *Turn off Lakemont Boulevard on Cougar Mountain Way to 168th, which turns sharp right to become SE 60th. At 0.6 mile from Cougar Mountain Way turn steeply uphill right on Cougar Mountain Drive, traversing the slopes of Radio Peak 1 mile to the road-end at 1400 feet.*

For this loop, however, the trailhead is at Nike Park, where the missiles were in underground silos.

Directions: *Where Cougar Mountain Way turns sharp northeast to become 168th, go off south on 166 Way SE 0.7 mile to Nike Park, elevation 1200 feet. (As of 2002, a temporary gate stops cars sooner.)*

From Nike Park walk the Clay Pit Road (or trail, as it will become when the Newcastle Brick Plant ceases mining) a long ¼ mile and go off left on the Klondike Swamp Trail. Primevally this headwaters basin of Coal Creek held a lake a mile long and a thousand feet wide. A dam across the lower end increased storage capacity to 10 million gallons, the principal water supply for the mines. Perhaps partly due to leakage, but largely because of evaporation when the ancient forest was logged in the 1920s, the lake became the Klondike Swamp, a magnificent huge wetland certain to remain a wildlife refuge even in a future when the trails are thronged.

In a scant 1 mile from the road turn right on the Lost Beagle Trail, which ascends forest to the Army fence ringing Radar Park and follows the fence to the Shangri La Road-Trail, a few feet from the park entry and ¾ mile from the Klondike Trail.

Come here on an icy winter day to watch the winds pile snowdrifts that would do North Dakota proud. The biggest views—the

Seattle skyline and the Olympic Mountains from Cougar Mountain

airplane-wing views—are not inside the fence but across the entry road on the grassy knoll of the Million Dollar View. Had King County not bought the spot, that's how much would have been paid for it by the plutocrat builder of a trophy home, in views from Olympics to Cascades, Seattle to Bellevue, Lake Sammamish (a swan-dive below) to Mount Baker and the San Juan Islands.

Descend Shangri La Trail ⅛ mile and turn right on Tibbetts Marsh Trail. Quickly turn right on Anti-Aircraft (AA) Ridge Trail to a Y, where Lost Beagle Trail goes right; stay left down AA Ridge, through alder-maple forest, fir-hemlock-cedar forest, and enormous stumps of Douglas fir. A scant 1 mile from Shangri La is Cougar Pass, 1250 feet, the divide between Coal Creek and West Fork Tibbetts Creek. At the junction here the right fork leads ⅛ mile to the Klondike Swamp Trail. Turn left along the edge of Lame Bear Swamp, as formidably inaccessible to humans as a wetland gets. At ⅓ mile from Cougar Pass, the Tibbetts Marsh Trail is intersected. Turn right, go uphill ¼ mile, and emerge from woods to the wide-open spaces of the Clay Pit, 1375 feet.

The Clay Pit Road goes right 1 mile to Nike Park. (On the way find a short path left to a great big grate over an awesome hole in the ground.) But before leaving the pit, ascend the slopes (note black streaks—the Primrose Seam) to the top, a few yards from the wooded summit of Clay Pit Peak, 1525 feet. The views are out over the Sammamish basin and East Sammamish Plateau to the Cascades, from Pilchuck and Baker to Glacier and Index and Teneriffe and Si.

It is proposed that the notch cut in the impervious clay to drain the pit floor be dammed. Nature would then take care of creating a large lake-marsh, the terrain shaped to provide peninsulas and coves and wildlife-refuge islets. In no more than a decade the great blue herons would begin nesting.

WILDERNESS PEAK VIA SHY BEAR PASS

Round trip: 4 miles
High point: 1595 feet
Elevation gain: 1200 feet
Maps: 15, 16

The name, "The Wilderness," was not given lightly. This truly is a wildland, partly railroad-logged in the 1920s and cat-logged in the

This is perhaps the quietest nook of the Cougar Mountain Regional Wildland Park. Blink your eyes, stamp your boot twice, and say, "I am in the heart of the North Cascades." And you are.

1940s, but in each case by a quick once-through, man's intrusion limited to a few days, nature then let alone to rebuild. Part never was logged at all, and the virgin forest of Douglas fir on the slopes of Wilderness Peak is as noble an assemblage of ancient snagtops and wolves as is to be found so near Seattle.

Directions: *Go off I-90 on Exit 15 and drive south on Highway 900 to the Newport Way stoplight. Continue on Highway 900 south 2.6 miles to the Wilderness Creek trailhead parking area. Elevation, 365 feet.*

The trail bridges Wilderness Creek and ascends switchbacks along the gorge, views down to waterfalls, across to a pair of tall, arrow-straight cottonwoods, and up through interlaced billows of maple to tiny fragments of sky. The creek is recrossed to a Y. Cliffs Trail goes right, in 1 mile attaining the summit of Wilderness Peak, 1595 feet, Cougar Mountain's highest point; go left to The Boulders, house-size chunks of fern-covered volcanic rock fallen from cliffs plucked over-steep by the Pleistocene ice. Far enough for a picnic lunch in the green gloom of handsome big trees, beside the splashing creek. In summer, 20 degrees cooler than outside.

The way recrosses the creek and swings away from it in switchbacks on slopes of Ring Road Peak. At an unsigned split go right, through a bottom and over the creek to the fabled under-a-boulder Cougar Mountain Cave, sleeping room for three bobcats or one bear. A long board-walk enters the boggy flat of Big Bottom. To this point there have been a few stumps from the high-grading done by the gypos, not enough to mar the feel of pristinity. Now, on the slopes of Wilderness Peak, there are no stumps at all, an unmolested ancient forest of Douglas fir.

The ear notes to its surprise that sounds of automobiles and quarry and all-around civilized hubbub have mysteriously muted. Amid the forests, which are half virgin and full virgin, the surrounding peaks have blocked out the chattering simian world. This is perhaps the quietest nook of the Cougar Mountain Regional Wildland Park. Blink your eyes, stamp your boot twice, and say, "I am in the heart of the North Cascades." And you *are*.

Beyond and above the fern-hung maples and big hemlocks of Beautiful Bottom, at 1¼ miles, is Shy Bear Pass, 1320 feet.

Straight ahead, Shy Bear Trail descends to Cabbage Creek, in 1½ miles reaching Far Country Lookout and then continuing to Indian Trail; another fork leads to Fred's Railroad.

To the left, Long View Peak Trail attains that summit in a scant ½ mile and proceeds via Doughty Falls and the Skunk Cabbage Farm and Malignant Deceiver Ridge to the Far Country.

To the right, Wilderness Peak Trail ascends a scant ½ mile to the summit. Linkage to the Wilderness Cliffs Trail enables a looping return via Wildview Cliff and Big View Cliff.

There is no view from Wilderness Peak. The Douglas firs growing here were perhaps half-a-century old when the gypos came through and weren't big enough to bother with. But now they're getting on to the century mark. A few steps away is where the gypos quit and the virgin ancient forest begins. When clouds slide through, dimming the trees to Platonic essences, or snowflakes float through white-sagging branches, who needs to see Southcenter?

SQUAK MOUNTAIN STATE PARK
Maps: 18

Squak is where the Alps began, before they were the Alps. Way back in the 1960s the Bullitt family bought 500 acres of the summit area as a country retreat. In 1972, deciding the green wildness was too much wealth to be hogged, that the Public Trust Doctrine required it to be made plainly public, the family shopped around for a suitable public manager. The only game in town appeared to be Washington State Parks. However, all too aware of that agency's predilection for paving and mechanizing, the Bullitts' deed of gift stipulated no logging, no management roads, no wheeled machines, not even any horses, the park to be kept "forever wild." Miffed by these handcuffs on managerial hands, State Parks so ignored the Natural Area that it became a regional motorcycle-jeep playground. Ultimately, however, the Issaquah Alps having been created, the Trails Club raised such a stink about the malfeasance and misfeasance that noses wrinkled from Seattle to Olympia.

A King County bond issue in 1989, followed by a state wildlife habitat bond issue, a further gift from the Bullitts and a purchase by the City of Issaquah, have brought the State Parks and contiguous King

County Parks and Issaquah Parks holdings to better than 2500 acres—not a "forest gymnasium," but a "wildland museum." No wheels.

The mountain's trails (many of which are called "roads" because that is what State Parks illegally allowed them to be) can be walked from trailheads on every side. Most elaborate and least used is the (late-coming) State Parks blacktop-and-privy on the May Valley Road. Highway 900 has a pair of unofficial trailheads popular with the experienced, not really recommendable to the newcomer, and the major trailhead of the future (but not yet), the abandoned Sunset Quarry, which has been purchased by Issaquah Parks. The two trailheads directly from Issaquah, "Trailhead City," are the favorites.

Squak Mountain trail

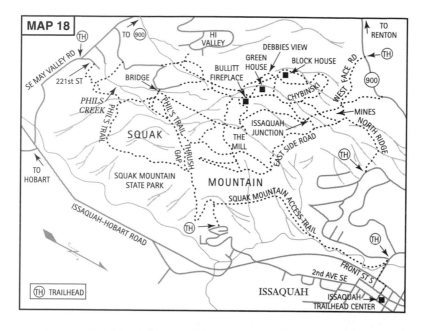

MAP 18

TO RENTON

TO (900)

HI VALLEY

DEBBIES VIEW

GREEN HOUSE

BLOCK HOUSE

BULLITT FIREPLACE

SE MAY VALLEY RD

221st ST

BRIDGE

CHYBINSKI

WEST FACE RD

(900)

PHILS CREEK

PHIL'S TRAIL

PHIL'S TRAIL

MINES

NORTH RIDGE

SQUAK

THRUSH GAP

ISSAQUAH JUNCTION

THE MILL

EAST SIDE ROAD

MOUNTAIN

TO HOBART

SQUAK MOUNTAIN STATE PARK

SQUAK MOUNTAIN ACCESS TRAIL

ISSAQUAH-HOBART ROAD

FRONT ST S

2nd AVE SE

ISSAQUAH

ISSAQUAH TRAILHEAD CENTER

(TH) TRAILHEAD

BUS-TO-SQUAK TRAIL

One way: from Trailhead Center to East Side Trail 1¼ miles
High point: 1300 feet
Elevation gain: 1150 feet
Map: 18

When the Issaquah Alps Trails Club commenced in the late 1970s, it trumpeted to the masses, which were grimly aware of the coming obsolescence of unrestricted "freedom of the wheel," the stirring message "WILDERNESS ON THE METRO." As bus service increases to meet our society's needs for reliable transportation, a number of trailheads in the Issaquah Alps will indeed provide convenient public access from homes throughout the Metro service area. One trailhead now exemplifies the concept most brilliantly.

Directions: *In Issaquah, get off the bus on Bush Street, at the Trailhead Center, replica (except for modern plumbing) of the stationmaster's house of the 1890s. Elevation, 150 feet.*

Even if arriving by car, this is the place to start because parking is ample here and is very constricted farther along. Study the map in the kiosk outside the building (and reproduced in these pages). The first

Ferns along Squak Mountain trail

half-mile of the route is along Bush, then Front, then Coal Mine Road—and for the last bit through a neighborhood before plunging into the woods will make you wish you'd spent more time studying the map. (Trail signs are sometimes missing.)

The foot-only path crosses one last street, Sunrise, and from then on is steadily, moderately up for 0.8 mile (says the sign) in all the lushness of Squak's forest, second-growth but old, dating from the era of bullteams and steam donkeys.

The East Side Trail, intersected at 1300 feet, leads in both directions to all the good stuff (and more) described in the trip following this.

CENTRAL PEAK–NORTHEAST FACE LOOP

Loop trip: 5 miles
High point: 2000 feet
Elevation gain: 1000 feet
Map: 18

Even when it was being polluted and pounded by a parade of snorting machines razzing the primitive roads, this was the classic Squak walk. Now that State Parks is enforcing the law as commanded by the Bullitts, it is more so. The high elevation of the trailhead makes for the easiest of trips—as well as meaning that if white is seen on the summit trees while driving by on I-90, parents know the quickest way to take their kids to a snowball fight.

Directions: *Drive west from downtown Issaquah on Sunset, past the fish hatchery, to the stoplight. Proceed straight through the intersection onto Mountain Park Boulevard and follow its twists and turns steeply uphill 0.6 mile. Turn left on Mountainside Drive 0.2 mile, then right on Idylwild. Drive 0.2 mile to a blockaded dead-end stub, elevation 1000 feet.*

Clamber over the wheel-blocking boulders to a large readerboard, "Squak Mountain State Park Natural Area *foot only.*" The Bullitt Access Trail, as the state's trail signs call what we knew for years as the North Ridge Road, leads 1 mile to Issaquah Junction, 1275 feet. The junction is of three road-trails: the North Ridge, the East Side (make mental note, this is the return leg of the loop), and the West Face from Highway 900.

(I have to go into parentheses about the West Face, my favorite Squak walk until speedway traffic on skinny old 1920s pavement freaked me out. I most strongly recommend the upper part as a side trip from Issaquah Junction, descending through big old firs and hemlocks. Creeks splash down green gulches. Fairy bells and columbine line the way, and swordfern and lady fern and licorice fern and maidenhair fern.)

Continue on the North Ridge Road ¼ mile to a junction, 1400 feet, and go off left on Lower Summit Road, which curves south, in and out of forest vales, a joy. At 1700 feet a side road climbs right a short distance to the Bullitt

> *Creeks splash down green gulches. Fairy bells and columbine line the way, and swordfern and lady fern and licorice fern and maidenhair fern.*

Fireplace, all that remains of their summer home. Continue straight ahead on Lower Summit to Central Peak, 2½ miles, 2000 feet, and a thicket of radio towers.

Views would be meager were it not for slots cut in the forest to let microwaves in and out. One gives views of May Valley, Cougar Mountain, Renton, Lake Washington, Puget Sound, Vashon Island. Another shows Lakes Sammamish and Washington, Bellevue, the Space Needle, and Mount Baker. To the south is a screened view of the Cedar Hills Garbage Dump, Enumclaw, and Rainier.

Don't turn around just because you've bagged the peak—loop onward, the best of the trip lies ahead. Descend the service road a short bit to 1925 feet and turn left on the Summit Trail, a lovely wild-land path down a ravine of lush mixed forest. At a scant 3 miles from trip's start is Thrush Gap Junction, 1500 feet, in the notch between Central Peak and Southeast Peak. Turn left, north, on Phil's Trail,

Fireplace is all that is left of the Bullitts cabin on Squak Mountain

which has the width of a narrow-gauge rail grade, such as those on Cougar and Tiger. But Squak's forests were not extensive enough to finance railroads. It got narrow-gauge trucks, primitive Macks and chain-drive Reos able to cling to cliffs on skinny gouges. As it was, the gypos high-graded more forests than they clearcut and left large sections strictly alone; the mountain has more virgin timber than any patch of land so close to downtown Seattle.

At little A Creek (named for the first initial of the name of a daughter of Bill Longwell, who walked thousands of miles on Squak before transferring affections to Tiger) are (if still there?) stringers of an old bridge, fern gardens in the air. The trail contours, blasted from andesite cliffs, a wonderful stroll in ginger, Solomon's seal, and oak fern, with screened views out to Issaquah and Tiger Mountain.

At a scant 3½ miles the trail abruptly ends on the crest of a spur ridge, 1600 feet. Traces of grade go out on the spur a few feet. Here, high above the valley, a portable sawmill operated—a "tie mill," carted around on a truck, to square small trees for railroad ties. Another surprise: a view—not of the expected Issaquah but over Cougar Mountain to towers of downtown Seattle.

Plunge down the woods, quickly hitting the East Side Road at 1300 feet. Turn left and contour around tips of spur ridges, into an alder-maple ravine, by windows out on the valley to complete the loop at Issaquah Junction.

TIGER MOUNTAIN STATE FOREST: THE WORKING FOREST

Map: 19

As Caesar said of Gaul, Tiger Mountain is divided in three parts. The hiker may well wonder why it is that we, here, are taking them up by inverse order of hiking popularity, beginning with the one in which trail recreation coexists with commodity production—the "working forest" as contrasted to what might be thought of (insufficiently, by the way) as the "recreation forest," where trails never will have to compete with logging trucks. The latter is the subject of the two following sections.

The reason we are doing it this way is to stress that the motivation for creating the Tiger Mountain State Forest was not (repeat,

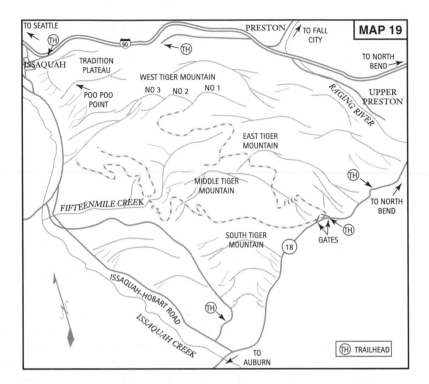

MAP 19

TO SEATTLE
PRESTON
TO FALL CITY
TO NORTH BEND
ISSAQUAH
TRADITION PLATEAU
WEST TIGER MOUNTAIN
NO 3   NO 2   NO 1
POO POO POINT
RAGING RIVER
UPPER PRESTON
EAST TIGER MOUNTAIN
MIDDLE TIGER MOUNTAIN
FIFTEENMILE CREEK
TO NORTH BEND
SOUTH TIGER MOUNTAIN
18
GATES
ISSAQUAH-HOBART ROAD
ISSAQUAH CREEK
TO AUBURN
TH TRAILHEAD

not) to make a State Park. Indeed, the State Forest never could have been established had not the commodity production/jobs provision/tax revenues of the forest industry been maintained. To be sure, the "workings" of this particular forest constitute an evolutionary leap toward a forest industry with a firm future, but the hiker must find his/her pleasure alongside the logger doing his job.

However, in this working forest, as contrasted to those of private industry, the logger views the hiker not as intruder but companion. To see the difference, go out into the bleak vastness of the horizon-to-horizon clear-cuts of the Weyerhaeusers.

With that philosophical prologue, on into history:

The "tiger" may have been: the cougar, mountain lion, catamount; the tiger lily which blooms so gaudily in late spring; a Scots word, *taggart*, meaning, rocky; or a rocky Scot named Taggart. In Issaquah it used to be called Issaquah Mountain; in Preston, Preston Hill.

During the last third of the nineteenth century, bullteam loggers cut the giant cedars and Douglas firs of the lower slopes. Their careless fires and the blazes set by settlers to clear the land for hops and cows ran wild up the mountain. In the 1920s railroad loggers arrived, based at three mills. From the Hobart mill they built a trail of rails angling upward across the west slopes to Fifteenmile Creek and ascending its valley to the summit ridge. From the High Point mill they engineered the "Wooden Pacific Railroad," a tramway that went straight up the fall line to the 1900-foot level, where a rail grade was gouged on the contour around the jut of West Tiger Mountain, through Many Creek Valley, to a dead end at Poo Poo Creek. From the Preston mill a series of switchbacks climbed to the summit ridge. (Historians are investigating whether there were, in addition, a mill and rail lines from Kerriston.)

The "lokies" began to quit the mountain in the crash year of 1929 and by the middle 1930s had moved elsewhere, picking up their rails and ties to carry away with them. Tiger was abandoned to the new-growing forests, the wild creatures, the occasional hunter, and a scattering of moonshiners. The sole human structures on high were a state fire-lookout tower atop East Tiger and an airway beacon on West Tiger.

But there were hikers. The rail grades provided a network of routes to nearly every corner of the mountain. The boots of local folk pounded out accesses from their homes to the high country. The state trail to the fire lookout was walked by city folk who knew nothing more of the trail system; when the trail was replaced by a service road, they accepted that as equally serviceable for feet. Recreationally speaking, modern times came to Tiger—with a jolt—in 1966 when The Mountaineers put the service road in their epochal book, *100 Hikes in Western Washington.* Thousands upon thousands of urbanites learned to their delighted surprise that within minutes of their homes they could set out on a hike that would take them to a wild and alpinelike experience. The flood of hikers shared the road amicably with horses, with the few sturdy family cars ascending slowly (lest something get busted) to a picnic, and with the motorcycles of civil riders who chose that vehicle for the open-air freedom.

In the mid-1970s the idyll went sour. The family cars and the view-seeking motorcyclists were driven out by the 4x4s with roll bar and winch whose sport is "mud-running" and "snowcatting" and just plain slamming through the brush; the dirt bikes sans muffler, sans spark arrester, sans any feeling for nature except as something to mess up for ego's sake, whose sport is churning soil, muddying creeks, scaring the wits out of family-car drivers and hikers; the three-wheel and four-wheel ATVs, machines so dangerous they kill more of their drivers than they do hikers.

Further, in the mid-1970s the Weyerhaeuser Company, which in 1900 had acquired better than half the mountain from the Northern Pacific Land Grant, paying James J. Hill $6 an acre, or about $500,000 for its entire Tiger holdings, and had banked at least twenty-five times that amount through the first-round clearcutting, returned for a second barbecue. The State Department of Natural Resources, trustee-manager of nearly half the mountain, acting for a number of public-agency trusts (the largest being King County), prepared to follow suit. As the two commenced harvesting the virgin forests left by the railroad loggers, they opened new roads that instantly were taken over by the wheel-crazies and the gun-crazies.

By 1980 Tiger Mountain resembled a war zone. Bullets flew in

Mount Rainier from Tiger Mountain

every direction, despite the only legal shooting being during hunting season, and that with shotguns. To walk the roads was to risk being mugged or raped or at the least hazed and menaced. The police rarely could be talked into answering reports of crimes, saying that to safely venture onto the heights required a platoon of Marines.

But in 1980 the tide turned. A new State Lands Commissioner (head of the DNR), Brian Boyle, was elected. He came to the mountain, he saw, and in due time he arranged a land exchange that got Weyerhaeuser off the mountain (except for the summit ridge of West Tiger, where it retains lucrative tower colonies).

Finally, responding to a proposal by the Issaquah Alps Trails Club for an "urban tree farm," Commissioner Boyle proclaimed a Tiger Mountain State Forest of some 14,000 acres, managing it as a "working forest in an urban environment," to provide a continuous flow of forest products while serving as a laboratory to experiment with new ("kinder, gentler") forestry techniques compatible with the contiguity of Puget Sound City. Balanced consideration is given all, not merely some, forest products, a term here extended to wildlife habitat, pure water for fisheries and domestic consumption, preservation of the history of the forest industry, teaching of environmental sciences in the schools, research in forest sciences, and civil recreation, both on the roads and on the near-city, quiet trails.

Recreation goals have largely been reached. Some 52 miles of trails are freely open to feet; 14 other miles in the eastern sector of the forest accessed by Highway 18 are freely open to feet, horses, and bicycles; and 19 miles of gated management roads are freely open to feet, horses, and bicycles.

A selection of representative trails is described in these pages; for the full menu, see *Guide to Trails of Tiger Mountain State Forest*, by William K. Longwell Jr., published by the Issaquah Alps Trails Club.

TIGER MOUNTAIN TRAIL: SOUTH END

Round trip: to Hobart Gap waterfall 4 miles
High point: 1100 feet
Elevation gain: 600 feet
Map: 20A

Bill Longwell, Chief Ranger of the Issaquah Alps Trails Club, judges the north and south ends of the Tiger Mountain Trail to be the choicest bits of the 16-mile route. The north end is treated in the following section on the West Tiger Mountain Natural Resources Conservation Area. The lovely and easy south beginning is even better for legs very short or somewhat arthritic and shares with the whole of the way the (legal) freedom from harassment by wheels.

Directions: *Drive Front Street–Hobart Road 7.2 miles south from Sunset Way in Issaquah or a hoot and a holler north from the Highway 18 interchange and turn onto SE Tiger Mountain Road. In 1 mile, where parking is abundant on the wide shoulder to the left, spot the wide trail into the woods on the right. Elevation, 500 feet.*

A few steps in is a sign, "Tiger Mountain Trail. South Tiger Trail 1.5 miles." And another: "Hikers and Horses Only." The way begins on wide, mud-free tread, toddler-friendly, through big firs, then bigger maples, by an historic marker identifying the "Route of Woods-Iverson Railroad Grade." A steady little ascent culminates at a logging-road-become-trail; a sign says "West Side Road 3.7, Tradition Lake 16.0."

The way sidehills above a lush valley in virgin forest dating from a burn that got here before the loggers did. The Chief Ranger says in his footstep-by-footstep guidebook that this is "perhaps the loveliest section of the entire TMT." Giant sawn stumps begin, and the route becomes true trail and passes through Weedwhacker Gap, 1100 feet, and very shortly Hobart Gap, 1080 feet. Here the way meets a 1920s railroad grade. The left, the alternate TMT (part of the South Tiger Loop)

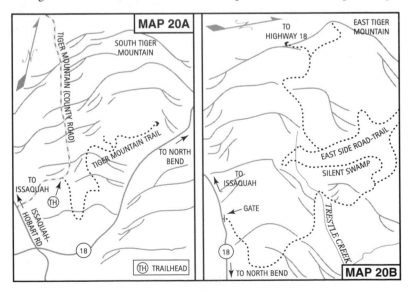

ascends a ridge of South Tiger Mountain (the summit, 2028 feet), crosses a 1700-foot pass, and drops past Otter Lake to the West Side Road. The right, the main TMT, contours on the rail grade along the opposite (east) side of South Tiger, crosses a powerline swath, and attains the West Side Road via a 1970s logging road closed to public vehicles.

Unless continuing on for the whole TMT, or intending the South Tiger Loop, a rewarding turnaround for an easy morning is a bit past Hobart Gap on the main TMT, a waterfall judged by the Chief Ranger to be Tiger Mountain's prettiest. Bring out the crackers and cheese, pickles and olives, jug of lemonade.

EAST TIGER MOUNTAIN VIA SILENT SWAMP

Round trip: to swamp 7½ miles, to summit 13½ miles
High point: at swamp 1550 feet; at summit 3004 feet
Elevation gain: to swamp 450 feet; to summit 2000 feet
Map: 20B

East Tiger is as high above the sea as Snoqualmie Pass, yet here it is, little more than several tosses of a Frisbee from the beach, often bringing winter from the Cascades to the heart of Puget Sound City. The walk to the summit (or waypoints, such as the Silent Swamp) is a favorite snowline-prober, the winter sport of folks who love the purity of crystalline white but despise expensive and clumsy encumbrances on their feet and cannot endure yodeling on the loudspeaker and fanny-waggling on the slopes.

Directions: *Drive Highway 18 to 3.1 miles west of I-90, 1.2 miles east of Holder Gap ("Tiger Summit"), and carefully make a treacherous turn off to a small parking space at a gated road, elevation 1100 feet.*

The three forest-management roads from Highway 18 (Tiger Mountain Road, West Side Road, and East Side Road) became popular walking routes when they were built in the late 1960s to middle 1970s, but automobile recreation by view-seekers and family picnickers soon grew so busy that foot travel could only be recommended on weekdays. Then the DNR, for reasons of vehicle safety and maintenance expense, was forced to permanently close all three roads to unauthorized motorized vehicles, which now are all-seasons, all-days joys to the nonmotorized public. The wildlife also rejoices, secure as it is from weapons-carriers/meat-wagons.

Listen now to frogs and wrens. Gape at huge stumps of cedar and fir. Admire devil's club and skunk cabbage of the lovely swamp.

At 2.4 miles from Highway 18 on the East Side Road is the lower end of the Silent Swamp Trail, elevation 1420 feet. Ascend a short bit to a railroad grade. Turn right on the grade, which makes a sweeping U-turn around the end of a low ridge, goes through a wide saddle at 1550 feet, and enters the valley of Silent Swamp. Hark! What is that new sensation that smites the ears? It is the sound of silence. The ridge has blocked out the din of I-90. Listen now to frogs and wrens. Gape at huge stumps of cedar and fir. Admire devil's club and skunk cabbage of the lovely swamp, headwaters of North Fork Trout Hatchery Creek.

The grade sidehills to a junction at 1 mile, 1700 feet, and a lesson in railroad history. Whereas the Hobart mill engineered its rail approach to Middle Tiger forests with a long, gradual sidehill ascent, and the High Point mill built a tramway up West Tiger, the Preston mill that operated on East Tiger employed switchbacks in this manner: A stretch of grade angled up a slope to a dead end. At the distance of one locomotive and a train of cars back from the dead end, the next stretch of grade took off uphill at an acute angle in the opposite direction. A train climbing the mountain proceeded past the junction to the dead end, pulled by the locomotive. A switch was thrown and the train went into reverse and backed up the next stretch, pushed to another dead end by the locomotive, which on the next switchback again took the lead.

On the route thus far, the Silent Swamp Trail where first intersected had just completed a switchback from the stretch of grade now occupied by the East Side Road. The sweeping U-turn was used to obviate the need for one switchback. Here at 1700 feet is the next switch. The grade reverse-turning to the right leads ¼ mile to the East Side Road at 1850 feet—and another switchback, along the road.

Ignoring the switchback at 1700 feet, proceed straight ahead on meager tread along and across the creek, then up the fall line to the dead end of a washed-out logging road. Turn right, back across the creek, returning to the East Side Road at 1950 feet, 1¾ miles from where it was left for trail. The road climbs steadily, swinging around the side of the 2786-foot satellite peak of East Tiger; views begin to open through young firs whose crowns are leaping up to block views.

The road tops the saddle between the peaks and drops a bit to join the Crossover Road, an offshoot of the Tiger Mountain Road, at 2670 feet, 6 miles from Highway 18.

The final ¾ mile is packed with entertainment. The Spring, source of the Spring Fork of Raging River: Ponder where it gets its year-round flow, here so near the summit. The sky, which now grows enormously as trees shorten. Though there is never a single 360-degree panorama, views extend in every direction as the road winds south, west, north, west, and south again so confusingly that a hiker needs a compass to avoid mistaking Duvall for Seattle. At one time or another look over the Raging River to Rattlesnake Mountain and the Cascades, over I-90 to Lake Alice Plateau, Snoqualmie Valley, Glacier Peak, and Baker, south to Rainier and the ruins of St. Helens, and over Middle Tiger to Seattle and The Whulge.

At 3004 feet the road flattens on the bulldozer-leveled summit, trashed with blabbertowers. A forest of huddled hemlocks blocks views north and east but horizons are open a hundred miles south and west.

NORTHWEST TIMBER TRAIL

Round trip: 5 miles
High point: 1800 feet
Elevation gain: 400 feet
Map: 20B

This trail, opened the summer of 1994, was built by the DNR for two reasons. First, few Tiger trails are on the Highway 18 side of the mountain, and that seems a recreational waste of some splendid country. Second, the new outdoor activity, riding off-pavement (fat-tire) bicycles, cannot be permitted on hiker/horse trails.

This trail and the also-new East Tiger Trail or Preston Railroad Trail (see Longwell's guide) are DNR experiments. As the only trails on the mountain open to wheels, they provide a laboratory to determine through actual use, rather than courthouse trial, where and how off-road bike routes might be provided, and if they can be provided without unacceptable damage to forest communities and the experience of other forest recreationists.

Directions: *Drive to Holder Gap ("Tiger Summit") on Highway 18 and park in the large lot, elevation 1100 feet.*

Walk the righthand of the two gated roads that start at the lot. In a

There is what has been called, aptly, "a Sargasso Sea jungle of moss-covered vine maples," an airy light-green interval.

short bit go off the road, right, on the signed trail. The forest is instantly superb and unfolds one after another display of what Nature can do in three-quarters of a century of good tree-growing conditions. The scattering of monster Douglas fir stumps is all that tells this is not a virgin forest, and one getting along smartly toward becoming ancient.

Every step, going and coming, is a delight. If climactic moments must be cited, there is what has been called, aptly, "a Sargasso Sea jungle of moss-covered vine maples," an airy light-green interval between the darker solemnities of big firs and hemlocks and cedars. A waterfall issues from a forest ravine to tumble over a wall of hard rock. Just beyond the falls and the High Bridge is the "Pre-Columbian," a Douglas fir some 40 feet in circumference. At trail's end is the East Side Road.

TIGER MOUNTAIN STATE FOREST: WEST TIGER MOUNTAIN NATURAL RESOURCES CONSERVATION AREA

As point group for the environmental coalition, the Issaquah Alps Trails Club participated in the citizens committee that aided the Department of Natural Resources in preparing the management plan for Tiger Mountain State Forest, published in 1986, a blueprint for preserving the market-driven forest industry from self-destruction, for developing and displaying a model by which the frontier past can be exchanged for a civilized future.

Throughout the years of citizen/DNR study and deliberation the Trails Club, while vigorously backing the working forest on Tiger (for which it had been arguing since 1979), urged that one sector of the mountain deserved priority for other social values than commodity production. In 1987 the state legislature authorized the DNR to set aside Natural Resource Conservation Areas to "protect outstanding examples of native ecosystems and habitat for endangered, threatened, and sensitive plants and animals." The DNR does not manage these areas for dollars but for non-monetary forest "products"—

including recreation (so long as it does not damage the other non-monetary products).

To date twenty-one such preserves have been established, the heart of what could be enlarged to a Washington State Wilderness System to complement the national system of the 1964 Wilderness Act. In 1989 the West Tiger NRCA became one of these; the final boundaries have not been settled, but at least 4400 acres are assured, making this "urban wildland" even larger than its companions on Squak and Cougar.

WEST TIGER 3

Round trip: 5 miles
High point: 2522 feet
Elevation gain: 2000 feet
Map: 21

The views from West Tiger are a classroom lesson in the geography of The Whulge country, spread out like an enormous relief map from Black Hills, Rainier, and the remnants of St. Helens on the south, Olympics west, San Juan Islands, Baker, and Shuksan north, and Cascades east, the saltchuck from The Narrows to Elliott Bay to Admiralty Inlet and Skagit Bay, cities from Tacoma to Seattle to Everett.

Of the West Tiger peaks, 3 is the lowest—and the best. It juts out farthest, hanging in the sky over downtown Issaquah, a swan-dive from Lake Sammamish. Burned naked by fires, blasted by cold storms in winter and hot sun in summer and vicious winds the year around, the thin soil barely covers bedrock andesite. Trees grow slow, pseudo-alpine. Spring brings mountain-meadowlike color of lupine, tiger lily, ox eye daisy, and spring gold.

Directions: *Go off I-90 on Exit 20 and turn right on the frontage road 0.4 mile to the gate, elevation 450 feet. If expecting to return after 7:00 p.m., when the gate is closed, park outside. If not, drive on 0.4 mile to the parking area at the Tradition Plateau trailhead, elevation 500 feet. If the area is full, return to the gate and park on the road shoulder outside.*

Though it may be said with some truth that "all trails lead to West Tiger 3," the most-used is the Tradition Trail. From the DNR Tradition Plateau trailhead, walk the Bus (Road) Trail a scant ¼ mile to a Y. Go left, soon turning steeply up from the plateau flat in mixed forest. The way winds and switchbacks, passes spurs left and right. Avoid confusion at a switchback just beyond a crossing of a creek, which trickles

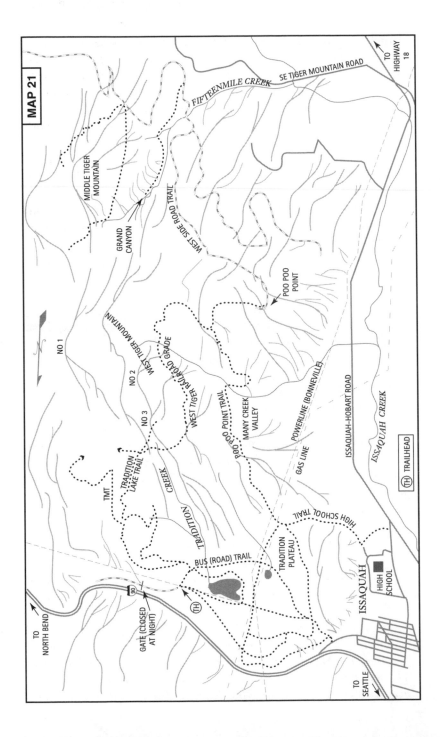

most of the summer; take the switchback left, re-crossing the creek.

At 1370 feet, a scant 1½ miles from the Bus (Road) Trail, the old logging road ends. Constructed trail turns up the fall line. In a long ½ mile is West Tiger Railroad Grade, 1900 feet. (On the way, avoid the slash in the forest made by Boeing to bury its powerline to the electronic gadgetry atop West Tiger 2; trail-runners use the slash to work off their problems and are a hazard to walkers.)

The trail crosses the grade and continues up, emerging from forest into views over Grand Ridge and the Snoqualmie Valley to the Cascades, and then proceeding through shrubs, over andesite rubble (or when winter winds blow from the North Pole, in drifted snow) up the ridge crest, at 2½ mile from the railroad grade reaching the summit, 2522 feet.

For a special treat, stay for the sunset over Puget Sound and the Olympics.

WEST TIGER RAILROAD

Loop trip: 10 miles
High point: 1900 feet
Elevation gain: 1400 feet
Map: 21

Between the era of logging that employed oxen and horses as pulling power, and modern logging with trucks, for several decades the railroad dominated the industry and tracks were laid throughout lowlands and foothills. Most grades have been converted to truck roads or otherwise obliterated. The longest remaining unmolested near Seattle is the West Tiger Railroad Grade, running 4 miles—the entire distance at an elevation of 1900 feet—from the north side of West Tiger Mountain around to the west, then south, in and out the enormous amphitheater of Many Creek Valley.

Directions: *Go off I-90 on Exit 20 and turn right on the frontage road 0.4 mile to the gate, elevation 450 feet. If expecting to return after 7:00 p.m., when the gate is closed, park outside. If not, drive on 0.4 mile to the parking area at the Tradition Plateau trailhead, elevation 500 feet. If the area is full, return to the gate and park on the road shoulder outside.*

From the Tradition Plateau trailhead, walk south 2½ miles on the Bus (Road) Trail, then the Bonneville powerline, to the upper terminus, 510 feet, of the Old State Road, which climbs here in 1 long mile,

Hang glider with West Tiger Mountain in background

gaining 325 feet, from Issaquah's Second Avenue at the backdoor of Issaquah High School. (This is a convenient trailhead for round trips to the huge views from Poo Poo Point.)

Climb andesite slabs across powerline and natural gas line to the forest edge, where two side-by-side former roads diverge up the steeps. Ascend the right into Many Creek Valley. At 1200 feet, 2½ miles from the powerline, the way in quick succession crosses a not-in-summer creek, all-year Gap Creek, and the deep, richly forested ravine of West Creek. A jumble of rotted logs tells of the one-time logging-truck bridge. Folks escape here from city turmoil on hot summer afternoons, sit beside the sparkling waters under marvelous big cedars, and eat a picnic supper in the wildness and the cool.

A bit beyond still another ooze of a creek the former road ends, at 1280 feet, and a trail sets out straight up the slope, going through a stand of ancient Douglas fir at 1500 feet. In a long ½ mile from the road-end, having gained 700 feet, the trail intersects the West Tiger Railroad Grade, 1900 feet, 5½ miles from the Tradition Plateau trailhead (3¼ miles from the high school).

To the right the grade dead-ends at the ravine of Poo Poo Creek and the trail continues ½ mile to Poo Poo Point, the most famous place name I've ever put on the map. (In the winter of 1976–77 there was heard in downtown Issaquah the haunting call of the Yellow-Shafted Talkie Tooter, the "poo! poo!" and "poo-poo-poo-poo-poo" by which the choker-setter talked to the yarder before the coming of cell phones. Thus was ushered in the Second Wave of clear-cutting, the cleanup of patches of virgin forest ignored by the First Wave of the 1920s. The loggers boast that mowing down the ancient trees on Poo Poo Point opened one of Tiger's finest views. Well, give Weyerhaeuser [then in charge around here] *that*. But this was not merely virgin forest, it was old growth. One observer commented, "If the company owned Seward Park, it would log that, too." Soon thereafter, the stumps of the old-growth trees mysteriously disappeared, too embarrassing to be left for ancient-forest photographers to document.)

For the loop, turn left on the grade and round a spur ridge into Many Creek Valley on a steep sidehill that gentles in the squishier, creekier center of the amphitheater. Note stringers of old bridges, mostly broken-backed and fallen, a few still intact, nurse-bridges growing ferns and hemlocks and candyflower in midair.

Having crossed West Creek at 1 mile and Gap Creek in ¼ mile more—the two largest of the eight or so (many) creeks—the grade

Issaquah, I-90, and Lake Sammamish from Poo Poo Point

curves onto steep south slopes of West Tiger. Now for something completely different: virgin forest of nobly large and tall Douglas firs, too small to interest loggers of the 1920s but sizable enough to give today's hikers a feeling for what the whole mountain was like a couple of human generations ago.

Trails are passed going up, going down (see Bill Longwell's guidebook). After 2½ miles on the rail grade, Tradition Trail leads down the mountain 2 miles to close the loop on the plateau.

Hikers who came upon the rail grade in the late 1970s were puzzled by the fact it connected to nothing. At both ends, dead ends. The mystery was explained by Fred Rounds, who when the weather was good used to emerge from the Newcastle mines to go logging on

Tiger. He explained to us newcomers how the "Wooden Pacific Railroad" connected the lumber mill (all remains obliterated by I-90) at High Point, elevation 450 feet, to the 1900-foot rail grade. Steam donkeys lifted rails and railroad cars and locomotive and loggers up this tramway and lowered tramcars loaded with the "big sticks" whose stumps are gaped at by hikers of today.

TIGER MOUNTAIN TRAIL: NORTH END

Round trip: 5 miles
High point: 1500 feet
Elevation gain: 1000 feet
Map: 21

October 13, 1979, was the official opening of the Tiger Mountain Trail, by then 7½ years in the thinking and 3½ in construction, occupying close to 300 person-days, costing a total in public funds of $0.00, and resulting in a 10½-mile route that subsequently was acclaimed by a foundation-sponsored group engaged in a tour of inspection from coast to coast as "the greatest near-city wildland trail in the nation." Subsequent relocations of the north and south trailheads have lengthened the distance to 16 miles. Along the way are broad and varied views, plant communities ranging from virgin fir to alder-maple to pseudo-alpine andesite barrens—a rich sampling of the good and great things of Tiger Mountain.

The idea for this masterpiece may be said to have been hatched at a Mountaineers meeting in 1972. However, the fledgling never would have gotten out of the nest had it not been taken under the wing of Bill Longwell, who chose the route and led hundreds of work parties—Mountaineers, Volunteers of Washington, Issaquah Alps Trails Club, youth groups, students at Hazen High School—and went out himself on countless solo "parties." Says Longwell in his definitive guidebook, "By late 1988 425 person-days, about 2000 hours, had gone into the trail. Finding a route took 40 trips. Then came 122 work parties. . . . " That was by summer of 1989. The work continues, under supervision of the DNR now.

The supreme hike of the Issaquah Alps is the TMT end-to-end from the (working) Tiger Mountain State Forest to its (wilderness) West Tiger NRCA, doing the entire 16 miles and 2200 feet of elevation gain (from the south trailhead) in a day, a good bit of exercise but in ordinary conditions (spring to fall) perhaps not overly taxing. The favorite method is a two-car switch, placing a car at the north trailhead, then driving to the south trailhead.

The trip is not recommended for every casual stroller to do on

Forest scene on Middle Tiger Mountain

his/her own. An experienced wildland navigator can find the way readily by consulting *Guide to Trails of Tiger Mountain* by (who else?) Bill Longwell, Chief Ranger of the Issaquah Alps. The inexperienced would do best to go on a trip guided by the Issaquah Alps Trails Club or The Mountaineers or other group. Hikers must keep in mind that in winter the snow may pile deep on the trail and in any season the clouds may blow wildly by. Fortunately, all along the route are escape hatches to lower and safer elevations; see the Longwell guide.

Directions: *Go off I-90 on Exit 20 and turn right on the frontage road 0.4 mile to the gate, elevation 450 feet. If expecting to return after 7:00 p.m., when the gate is closed, park outside. If not, drive on 0.4 mile to the parking area at the Tradition Plateau trailhead, elevation 500 feet. If the area is full, return to the gate and park on the road shoulder outside.*

The north end is a splendid round trip from the Tradition Plateau trailhead. Follow "TMT" signs from the restroom building to the Bus (Road) Trail, turn left on the West Tiger 3 Trail, and turn quickly left again on the TMT, signed "High Point Trail 2.4, West Tiger Railroad 4.4, Fifteenmile Creek 8.6, Middle Tiger 10.6, West Side Road 12.3, Hobart Road 16.0." The last of these is the south trailhead, the next to last the former trailhead before the extension past South Tiger.

The way sets out on the plateau flat in mixed forest grown rich and mellow since the railroad logging three-quarters of a century ago, then turns up to sidehill-gouge slopes of West Tiger 3. A rude slash in the wildness is crossed, the violence committed to bury the cable supplying power to Boeing's information superfreeway tower atop West Tiger 2. Mutter an oath and hurry on.

The trail climbs through alder-maple forest where post-logging regrowth has not yet brought the succession to conifers. Then, rounding a spur ridge, the alert hiker notes an absence of sawn stumps. The mood of the scene changes from deciduous light-and-airy to fir-hemlock shadowed-somber. In the main the trees are not large, obviously are young. Yet it is a *virgin* forest because a forest fire left too little to justify attention by 1920s loggers. But were it not now preserved in the Natural Resources Conservation Area, loggers would come a-running to mine out the scattering of near-ancient Douglas firs, which survived the blaze with no worse damage than a bit of charcoaling of the thick bark that renders these elders virtually fireproof. From "Anschell's Allee" (ask the Chief Ranger why he gave that name) sawn stumps resume, rotting corpses of monster ancients.

The route swings off the dry-forest spur ridge into the jungle wetness of a deep, wide canyon, where a major branch of High Point Creek is bridged. The tread swings up and out of the canyon, bridges the creek's main branch in a deeper, wider canyon, and just beyond milepost 13 intersects the High Point Trail.

The junction is far enough for a pleasant afternoon's lesson in the procession of forests from fire and/or logging to (or near) ancience. For quite a full day, see the Longwell guidebook (songbook, really), which carries on and up to the West Tiger Railroad, up more to the eyes-wide views from the slopes of West Tiger 2, and more from the highest point of the TMT, Manning's Reach, 2600 feet. Rest on the bench built for Manning by the Chief Ranger and return to the Tradition Plateau via the TMT or any of the looping alternatives.

TRADITION PLATEAU NATURAL RESOURCES CONSERVATION AREA
Map: 22

There was a glacier on the north, which in retreating dammed up a great lake. There was a river flowing from the east between Grand Ridge and Tiger Mountain, pushing a delta out into the lake. Glacier, lake, and river gone, the moraine was divided in two by a post-glacial stream. The half to the north became a gravel mine. The half to the south became the Tradition Plateau, providing water to the City of Issaquah from rainfall on Tiger Mountain, which sank into the moraine and gushed out in The Springs. When the city gave up The Springs in favor of wells, it entertained other possible uses of the ("in reserve") watershed. For a time the politicking was Marx Brothers comic opera. Finally the City Council sobered up and designated the city property a Tradition Lake NRCA, to be managed in conjunction with the West Tiger NRCA.

The plateau has become the most popular wildland walking area in the region. Its trails are easy to reach and easy to walk, well-groomed and mostly lakebed flat. They serve families with tots on parents' backs or toddling experimentally on their own feet, school classes studying the wild world, assorted pedestrians come to watch birds or sniff flowers. A wheelchair trail has been begun and will be extended. The powerline swaths welcome horses. The service roads give safe riding

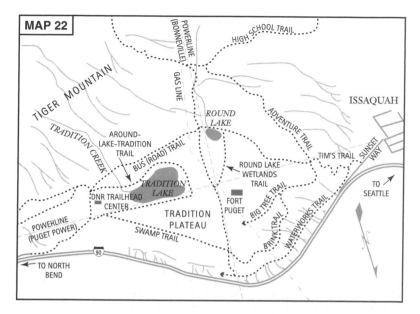

for children on bicycles. (Trails do not accept wheels, which initially were allowed on selected footpaths, proceeded very quickly to destroy them, requiring costly rebuilding and policing, and that was that.)

The trails are best served, for most people, by the Tradition Plateau trailhead (see the previous section for directions). However, the downtown Issaquah trailhead is superior for local residents, for visitors arriving by Metro bus, and for folks with glitzy cars that attract the bands of bandits native to I-90.

Directions: *From the (old) Issaquah city center on Front Street, get off the bus and walk east on Sunset to the uprise of Tiger, elevation 150 feet. Find Tim's Trail, paralleling the powerline swath, and climb steeply to the brink of the Lower Plateau, 425 feet.*

I will not, here, give directions to the eight (or more) trails on the plateau. For these, see Longwell's guidebook. Or not—the map herein and numerous trail signs make routefinding simple. Choose any (or all) of the following for a lazy afternoon or several busy days:

Tradition Lake, circuit loop 1½ miles. It's a lake—need I say more? Groves of halfway-ancient cedar and fir, birdsongs, floating ducks, perching eagles, pond lily in yellow bloom, lodges of the beaver who lived here until they ate up all the salad trees.

Bus Trail/Puget Trail, loop trip 2 miles. Among mementoes of the agricultural past on a 130-acre homestead are apple trees that are

Round Lake

top-pruned by bears, and what was, before it became a chicken house, a 1940-or-so Greyhound Scenicruiser. The Nook Trail is passed, leading to the fabled Tiger Mountain Caves. The loop is completed on the powerline paths we lump together as the "Puget Trail," which passes the walled substation we know as "Fort Puget."

Swamp Trail, ½ mile. Tradition Lake has no surface outlet. Its seepage flows through an aquifer under the powerline swath, emerging on the Lower Plateau. Swamp flowers, wet-loving birds, browsing elk.

Round Lake Wetlands, one way ¾ mile. Another lake! At least until winter's rain seeps underground or evaporates. But the wetland forest stays perennially wet. Semi-ancient Douglas fir but also water-greedy cottonwood, in late fall bursting into yellow flame.

Adventure Trail, one way ¾ mile. A construction by the outdoor club of Pine Lake Middle School, off the Lower Plateau, up and down, to the Old State Road. Little ridges cut by little vales.

Big Tree Trail, one way ½ mile. An afternoon is not enough. Examine the path for tracks and signs of coyote, cougar, deer, bear, raccoon. Sit on a mossy log beside the swamp, through which water moves ever so slowly and quietly, enjoy the blossoms of lily-of-the-valley, and fill lungs with skunk cabbage. See eight species of fern and scores of mosses and lichens and liverworts. Hear the winter wren and varied thrush. The wildland arboretum has two unique features, as well. A stretch of cedar puncheon dating from the 1880s is the area's only known surviving bullteam skid road, along which oxen dragged the "big sticks." So much time has elapsed that trees then too small to interest loggers have grown to noble dimensions, a rainforest mix of Douglas fir, Sitka spruce, hemlock, cedar, and fern-hung maple. Some Douglas firs were too large for the bullteams—one measures 24 feet in circumference and has been found by coring to be 1100 years old.

Brink Trail, one way ¾ mile. A path follows the brink of the Lower Plateau above a series of gulches where devil's club and salmonberry are so densely interwoven, soil so knee-deep mucky, that neither from the brink above nor the Waterworks Trail below can an explorer sanely venture. Where the wild things are. One afternoon, returning from a solo work party, I found my brand-new construction ratified by seals of approval by a deer, a coyote, and a bear. Waterfalls tumble unseen down the jungle from the plateau aquifer to East Fork Issaquah Creek, almost drowning out I-90, whose civilized din enhances the "wildness within."

Waterworks Trail, round trip 2 miles. The underground reservoir that was Issaquah's water supply until construction of I-90 empties through an aquifer capped top and bottom by impervious layers of clay-rich sediments. At the scarp cut by the East Fork

One afternoon, returning from a solo work party, I found my brand-new construction ratified by seals of approval by a deer, a coyote, and a bear.

they seep out, trickle out, and gush out—one spring after another for half a mile. The larger of them pass through concrete filtration boxes formerly connected to the city's main water tank, now removed. Issaquah kids with an attachment to historical roots come here on summer-day pilgrimages to drink the waters, declaring, "You just don't get water like that from city pipes."

Big Tree Trail

Tim's Trail, one way ¼ mile. At a turnout a bit past the easternmost homes on Sunset Way, a volunteer-built staircase ascends to the abandoned railroad grade just short of where a long trestle used to cross the valley of East Fork Issaquah Creek. Walk left several steps to the start of the path, built by former Issaquah Councilman Tim O'Brian, ascending a narrow ridge beside a deep gorge. Ancient forest! Within Issaquah city limits!

STILL MORE ALPS
Map: 23

East of Tiger, beyond the Raging River, is the connector to the Cascades, 3500-foot Rattlesnake Mountain. A new Rattlesnake Mountain Scenic Area of 1777 acres, eventually to be enlarged to some 3000 acres, is jointly administered by King County Parks and the State Department of Natural Resources under the regulations (though not the name) of a Natural Resources Conservation Area.

Rattlesnake is treated in our *55 Hikes Around Snoqualmie Pass: Mountains to Sound Greenway.* The trails are incompletely surveyed there because a management plan not yet finished will reshape the trail system, at present much the same as when I described it in my *Footsore 2* of 1979. Rattlesnake Ledge, the scenic superstar, is now, as when I first made an illegal (then) ascent in 1952, the big show of the North Bend area.

South of Tiger, beyond Highway 18, is the connector to the Cedar River Watershed, 2602-foot Taylor Mountain. In 1997 King County Parks acquired 1700 acres for a King County Forest. Though the Green Trails map for Tiger Mountain shows the old logging roads that have been taken over for trails, these are not the system of the future. The management plan is not expected to be completed until 2003, fully implemented for another half-decade. The unofficial interim entry is on Issaquah-Hobart Road (276 Avenue SE) about ¼ mile south of Highway 18, at SE 188 Street, elevation 550 feet. The trails will follow 5 miles on or near banks of Holder and Carey Creeks to a high point of 2000 feet.

North of Tiger, beyond I-90, is 1400-foot Grand Ridge, which since my first *Footsore* guidebooking there in 1977 has become such a dark and bloody ground of plundering developers and screeching fat-tire warriors I don't even like to think about it. But must, because King County Parks has 1250 acres for a new Grand Ridge Park, more in

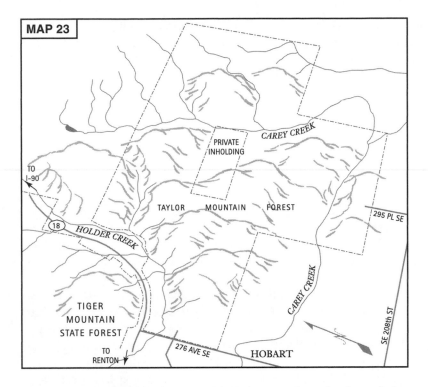

MAP 23

CAREY CREEK

PRIVATE INHOLDING

TO I-90

TAYLOR   MOUNTAIN   FOREST

295 PL SE

18   HOLDER CREEK

CAREY CREEK

TIGER MOUNTAIN STATE FOREST

SE 208th ST

TO RENTON

276 AVE SE   HOBART

"Section 36 park," and the State DNR has another chunk, and the master-planning is like trying to cook a pot of pottage amid a pack of snapping jaws—did I mention the soccer Nazis?

In some future edition of this book I'll have to come to grips but just now my brain hurts.

OTHER TRIPS

See books and maps published by the Issaquah Alps Trails Club:

Cougar Mountain Regional Wildland Park, Coal Creek Park, and May Creek Park, by Charles McCrone. A foreword contains "How We Got the Park," by Harvey Manning.

Guide to Trails of Tiger Mountain State Forest, a book and map by William G. Longwell Jr.

Opposite: *Cedar River Park*

CEDAR RIVER

CEDAR RIVER

Management: Renton Parks, King County Parks
Topographic maps: USGS Mercer Island, Renton, Maple
Valley, Black Diamond, Hobart—and their equivalents in the
Green Trails series, privately published

Puget Sound City's most useful river, bringing clean mountain water
from the Cascade Crest to faucets, flushing Lake Washington, giving
salmon a route from the ocean to spawning grounds.

Elevations below the level of winter white, trails mostly flat.

The Cedar is not only a reservoir of domestic water but also the
reservoir of wildlife that makes Puget Sound City the world's largest
city adjacent to so large a population of birds and beasts that never have
to fret about getting shot. The 103,000-acre Cedar River Watershed,
closed to the public, is the reason there are cougar on Cougar Mountain, elk through May Valley nearly to Lake Washington, and lynx and
coyote and bear and bobcats dining on pussycats. To be sure, the closure denies their favorite recreation to those humans for whom "wildlife" means something to eat.

Shooting is just one intrusion of violence into wildlands. The fish-
erman storming paths to the riverbank, the hiker pounding the trail,
throngs of bicyclers yipping and giggling at high speed, the family

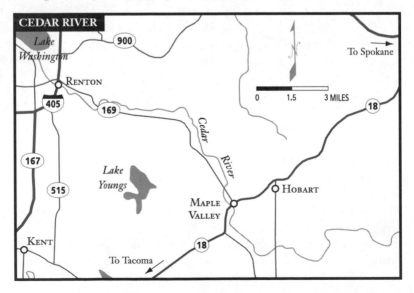

Gene Coulon Memorial Beach Park

circus spreading a blanket on the ground for a picnic lunch are, in sum, the equivalent in wild eyes of a Panzer division of motorcycles carrying attack rifles. So let us let the beasts be and take our pleasure outside their sanctuary. If we were allowed in with our boots, the rest of mankind would clamor for equal rights for their wheels and toys. Already bikeways are being penciled in on wish lists. Golly knows mankind has virtually the entire planet, lands and waters and skies, open to its violence. The wild creatures are running out of places to take a nap.

GENE COULON MEMORIAL BEACH PARK

Round trip: 3 miles
High point: 50 feet
Elevation gain: none
Map: 24

What man has put asunder, man may sometimes have a chance to put back together. Renton Parks started with 57 acres of Lake Washington shore hemmed in by railroad tracks and mucked up industrially for a century. Guided by a Jones & Jones design, it fashioned a park that on fine weekends swarms with swimmers, sunbathers, fishermen, canoeists, stinkpotters, sailboaters, and little kids yelling—but on weekdays is as peaceful a lakeshore as one could wish, only the goslings and ducklings making a racket.

Directions: *Go off I-405 on Exit 5, turn right on Park Avenue, then right on Lake Washington Boulevard North, then left into the park, elevation 25 feet.*

In an air distance of 1 mile are 1½ miles of in-and-out shore paths. For the full trip, park at the south end in a lot serving South Beach. Walk to the water, in panoramas that include the mouth of the Cedar River, Beacon Hill, the south end of Mercer Island, and a glimpse of Seattle towers.

Shore paths lead northward past the kids' playground, the bathing beach (enclosed by a concrete walkaround excellent for out-in-the-lake viewpoints), coots, ducks, and geese to a bridge over the marsh estuary of Johns Creek. A second parking lot serves the boatlaunch and boat harbor. The Lagoon is enclosed by the 1000-foot floating boardwalk of the Picnic Gallery. The Gazebo, the Pavilion, the Ivar's Eatery all are in turn-of-the-century architecture recalling the waterfront amusement parks of young Seattle.

Interface, a bronze sculpture by Phillip Levine, demands a pause. The shore continues along the largest enclosure, Log Boom Pond, logs moored at the outer edge to fend off razzerboats. Between water and railroad tracks are The Mount, a hummock that adds topographical interest, and a profusion of plantings of trees and shrubs, native and exotic.

At an entry road from Lake Washington Boulevard is the third and final parking area, serving the Canoe Launch and the North Beach, ½ mile more of pathway. Granite boulders have been installed on the shore, as well as old timbers recognized as being rudely handsome

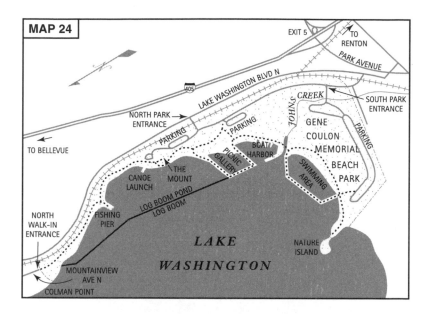

and rescued from the dump. The concrete piers and rotting pilings of a booming ground remain; here the railroad used to dump logs for rafting to mills. A bridge crosses Trestle Marsh (cattails and blackbirds). A fishing pier lets a person walk on the water.

CEDAR RIVER "TRAIL"

One way: from Lake Washington to Landsburg 22 miles
High point: 560 feet
Elevation gain: 535 feet
Maps: 25A–25D

This rails-to-trails victory is surely among the proudest achievements of the concept, and my only niggling objection is the abuse of the term "trail." It is the perfect exemplification of "multi-use travelway, nonmotorized," or, to stress its dominant use, "bikeway." It will be an even grander wheel route when hitched from Landsburg to the John Wayne multi-use travelway at Rattlesnake Lake, but this must not (NOT) be done

Across the river, a magic grotto where a creek falls free into the green from a tall wall of sandstones and shales.

through the Cedar River Watershed but by detouring around Taylor and Rattlesnake Mountains. Then, Daisy will look sweet upon the seat all the way from Lake Washington to Snoqualmie Pass, and ultimately to Idaho.

Directions: *Find the northern outlet of the Cedar River at the southern tip of Lake Washington in Renton, reached on the east side of the river from Riverside Drive.*

As a 2-mph pedestrian, a solitary, I enjoyed the route as trail the full 22 rail miles. Now I only recommend (highly) for walking several selected spots:

Near the river's outlet into Lake Washington (map 25A). Views over the Big Water to Beacon Hill, Queen Anne Hill, Mercer Island, and Cougar Mountain. Visions of the wild past. Primevally, the Black River drained from the lake hereabouts and flowed close beneath the steep slopes of Beacon Hill to join the Green River; somewhere in the middle of the plain that until recently became part of the lake during the rainy season, the Black was joined by the Cedar River, which later was diverted into Lake Washington.

Cedar River Park (maps 25A, 25B). At the mouth of the Cedar River valley—Maple Valley—look out to the Renton Plain, northern terminus of the Big (glacial) Valley.

Maplewood Golf Course (maps 25A, 25B). Wheelfree nature walks can total 2½ miles. At the upstream end of the golf course, go off the bikeway in the old farm. An entry lane winds to the river through fields that grow only grass, broom, tansy, and hellberry under the hungry eyes of hawks; something edible lives there, scurrying around in the weeds. The width of the fields so softens highway noise that the river drowns it out.

A forest of monster cottonwoods. Gravel bars. Across the river, a magic grotto where a creek falls free into the green from a tall wall of sandstones and shales, a seam of coal at the foot. In low water one can wade. A river meadow with a look across the water to a sand wall pocked by swallow caves.

Landsburg Bridge to Fort Pitt Bridge (map 25D). Don't go to Maple Valley at all. Drive Issaquah-Hobart-Ravensdale Road 3 miles south of Hobart to the Landsburg Bridge. Round trip to Fort Pitt Bridge, 4 miles.

Some weekends the kayakers stage slalom races in the river where it issues from the fenced watershed. Find a seat in the bleachers.

For 1 mile a trackside path downstream has long been beaten by

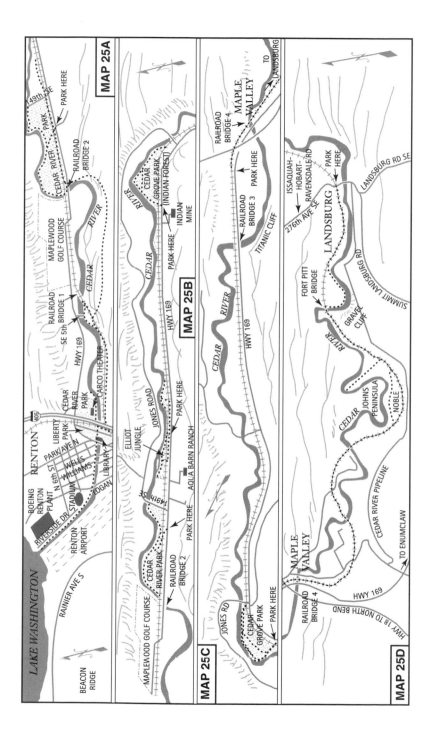

MAP 25A

LAKE WASHINGTON

BEACON RIDGE

RAINIER AVE S

RENTON

405

BOEING RENTON PLANT

RENTON AIRPORT

RIVERSIDE DR

LIBERTY PARK

CEDAR RIVER PARK

STADIUM

WELLS

WILLIAMS

N 6th ST

PARK AVE N

LOGAN

LIBRARY

CARCO THEATER

HWY 169

SE 5th ST

RAILROAD BRIDGE 1

MAPLEWOOD GOLF COURSE

CEDAR RIVER

CEDAR RIVER PARK

149th SE

PARK HERE

RAILROAD BRIDGE 2

MAP 25B

CEDAR RIVER

CEDAR GROVE PARK

HWY 169

JONES ROAD

PARK HERE

ELLIOT JUNGLE

149th SE

PARK HERE

AQUA BARN RANCH

PARK HERE (INDIAN FOREST)

INDIAN MINE

MAP 25C

MAPLEWOOD GOLF COURSE

CEDAR RIVER PARK

RAILROAD BRIDGE 2

JONES RD

CEDAR GROVE PARK

PARK HERE

CEDAR RIVER

HWY 169

RAILROAD BRIDGE 3

PARK HERE

TITANIC CLIFF

RAILROAD BRIDGE 4

MAPLE VALLEY

TO LANDSBURG

MAP 25D

MAPLE VALLEY

RAILROAD BRIDGE 4

HWY 18 TO NORTH BEND

HWY 169

JONES RD

CEDAR GROVE PARK

PARK HERE

CEDAR RIVER PIPELINE

TO ENUMCLAW

CEDAR RIVER

NOBLE

JOHNS PENINSULA

GRAVEL CLIFF

FORT PITT BRIDGE

SUMMIT LANDSBURG RD

LANDSBURG

276th AVE SE

ISSAQUAH-HOBART-RAVENSDALE RD

LANDSBURG RD SE

PARK HERE

fisherfeet. Branch paths lead to overlooks of dippers and ducks, mossy nooks among the maples, and picnic bars. On my first survey, in early October, there were a gull or heron on every boulder, squadrons of ducks on patrol, raptors circling above, and pools so full of sockeye salmon they scarcely left room for the water.

Where the grade enters an odd little valley, turn off on a riverside path that follows the stream around a big loop for ⅔ mile (the railroad shortcuts to the end in ⅓ mile). Enchantment! Virgin-looking forests

Cedar River Park

of big old conifers. Groves of giant cottonwoods. Understory of vine maple in flame (in October). And across the river the Great Gravel Cliff rising an absolutely vertical 150 feet from the gulls. A good turnaround is the bridge signed "Fort Pitt Bridge Works Pittsburgh PA 1890."

ECHO MOUNTAIN (LAKE DESIRE–SPRING LAKE REGIONAL WILDLAND PARK)

Round trip: 3 miles
High point: 899 feet
Elevation gain: 400 feet
Map: 26

Narrowly rescued from a "planned community" of 900 homes by the King County open-space bond issue of 1989, these 371 acres have been described as a "little Cougar Mountain." That is to say, a *wild-land*, not a gymnasium, but a museum. In the midst of suburbia. All the better.

Directions: *Drive 196 Avenue SE from Maple Valley Highway to SE 183rd. Turn right, then immediately right again on Spring Lake Drive 1 mile to the road-end gate, elevation 490 feet.*

Side trails lead out in every direction to dogs announcing the edge of private property. When you're barked at, turn back. The basic trip is to the summit. The forest on the way has had nearly a century to grow tall and cool-shadowed since the loggers went away. And—oh!—the summit bald, the sedimentary rock rounded and scraped clean by that old Canadian glacier. Deep-forest flowers yield to rock-slab flowers. There are even some views—Rainier and Tiger.

The Main Trail to the water tank serving local homes rarely is traveled by service vehicles. It sets out from the gate (just past a Wildlife Department boat launch on Spring/Otter Lake) parallel to a woods path that soon joins Main Trail. Salmonberry, bleeding heart, candyflower, trillium, avens. The woods path continues straight ahead, eventually leading out of the park.

Main Trail horseshoe-bends

Reflect on the succession displayed here: glacier-edge icewater lake to marsh to bog to meadow to forest.

right and climbs from the valley bottom of big cottonwood and cedar. At 590 feet, a trail (onetime road) goes left a scant ½ mile to a narrow sliver of park, "Lunch Beach," on Lake Desire. Watch for otters at play or beavers at work. And/or the nesting pair of bald eagles. Great blue heron or osprey.

At 738 feet Main Trail goes a short bit straight ahead to dead end at the water tank. Instead, turn right, steeply uphill, in blackberry and Solomon's seal, fairy bells and toothwort, out of the forest onto the rock bald. Walk softly! This summit area is very sensitive to human intrusion. Don't mash the flowers! In season for each, Easter lily (mid-April), chocolate lily (May), seablush, kinnickinnick, strawberry, monkeyflower, nodding onion. Serviceberry bushes are festooned with airy masses of light-green lichen.

Look out the open window through the trees. Expect to see Tiger. Instead, Rainier! But there also is Tiger, where Rainier ought to be. When sun is sparkling the water, see green-screened Lake Desire.

The serendipity of the park is the largest, most pristine (never mined for peat moss) sphagnum peat bog west of the Cascade-front vicinity. Do not—repeat, do not—stray from the plank walkway installed to keep feet on a nondestructive route. Reflect on the succession displayed here: glacier-edge icewater lake to marsh to bog to meadow to forest. The Labrador tea, swamp laurel (kalmia), cranberry, and sundew put on a fine bog flower show.

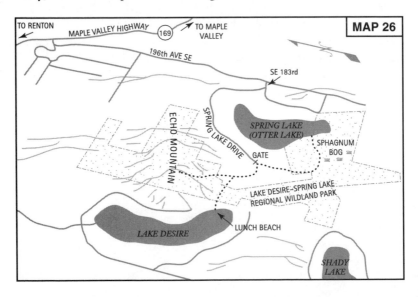

Lake Desire, Spring Lake Regional Wildland Park

Opposite: *Green River and Mount Rainier*

GREEN RIVER

GREEN RIVER

Management: State Parks, King County Parks, parks departments of "Big Valley City"
Topographic maps: USGS Renton, Maple Valley, Black Diamond, Cumberland, Eagle Gorge, Auburn, Des Moines, Poverty Bay—and their equivalents in the Green Trails series, privately published

Clean mountain water flows from the Cascade Crest to city faucets—of Tacoma. What's left over heads north through towns, farms, airplanes, and industry to Seattle. A little space remains for birds. Feet are pretty much out of it unless connected to wheels.

Elevations are closer to the sea than the sky, so whatever trails exist may be muddied by rain but hardly ever blocked by snow.

The Big River of Pleistocene time issued from the front of the Canadian glacier, engorged mountain tributaries, and flowed on south, seeking a way open to the ocean. Among the myriad legacies promi-

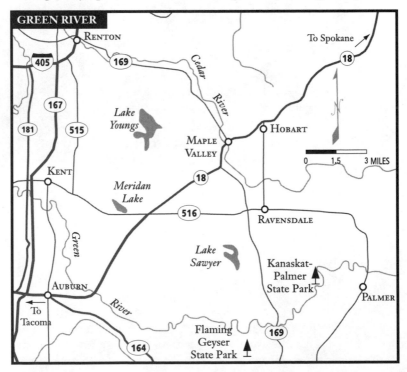

nent in the geomorphology of our Holocene time is the Big Valley extending south from the Seattle area to beyond Tacoma and Orting and, in a narrower version, to the Nisqually.

Streams very much smaller than the Big inherited its broad floodplain. When European settlers arrived, Mount Rainier's Puyallup entered the valley at Electron and turned north, at Orting picked up another Rainier river, the Carbon, and after a while turned west to Commencement Bay. A third Rainier River, the White, debouched in the Big Valley at Auburn during a dozen millennia, sometimes turned south to join the Puyallup and sometimes north to Elliott Bay. The farmers wearied of the fickleness and after a switch from north to south during a winter flood of 1906 called in the engineers to build dikes to fix it in that southward course. At the point of diversion, where it exits from the Cascade front, the river changes name to the Stuck—golly remembers why.

Some maps of pioneer days had the White entering Elliott Bay. Others called the river in its final stretch to Whulge the Duwamish, the Anglicized name of the local Original Inhabitants. Once the White was out of the picture, geographers were torn between Duwamish and Green, the latter being the old White's chief tributary, also entering the Big Valley at Auburn. The ultimate consensus was to keep the de-Whited river Green to its Tukwila junction with the Black, the outlet of Lake Washington, then make it Duwamish the rest of the way to the saltchuck. (For a time after the ice went away, the saltchuck, Whulge, occupied what is now the valley of the Duwamish, wrapped around the south end of Beacon Hill, and filled the trough north of Renton. Sedimentation by the White, at that time containing the Green and Cedar, dammed off Lake Washington and pushed Whulge around the corner and north to today's Elliott Bay.)

The primeval Black River was the sum of the Sammamish River, Juanita Creek, Thornton Creek, Kelsey Creek, Coal Creek, May Creek, Issaquah Creek, and all other waters of the Lake Washington basin. Less than a mile from the lake it received the Cedar River and thus snowmelt from the Cascades. It was a substantial stream, indeed, when it met the White River to form the Duwamish. Of course, it couldn't compete with the White's spring floods from The Mountain and would then reverse flow and pour Rainier water into the lake. The Originals therefore called it Mox La Push, meaning "two mouths." In 1912 the farmers diverted the Cedar into Lake Washington, from which its waters quickly exited in the Black. In 1916 the new Lake

Washington Ship Canal provided the lake a new outlet and the Black went out of the river business.

The riparian and human history of the Big Valley enlarges the pedestrian experience. The brown-black alluvium that fed Tacoma and Seattle, and the marshes that fed migrators on the Pacific Flyway, have largely vanished under blacktop and buildings. Flat ground, centrally located, is too expensive to grow food for man or beast or bird. The Big Valley has become the heavy-throbbing heart of Puget Sound City. Freeways rumble over the plain, unfruiting enough cropland to feed a Third World nation, and thunder up the valley walls. Jet airplanes rocket cloudward like so many Flash Gordons headed for Mongo and plummet forestward like so many gaudy baubles seeking Christmas trees, ceaselessly pummeling Puget Sound City with what the Port of Seattle and Chamber of Commerce hail as "the sound of progress" (money, that is).

DUWAMISH RIVER

A sewage pipeline from Renton to Duwamish Head is intended to accommodate a 12-mile nonmotorized travelway that may be interesting, or may not.

Directions: *From I-5 south, take Exit 156. Go north on Interurban Boulevard then right on 42 Avenue South. Go right at two consecutive flashing red lights, S 124 Street and 50 Place South. Just before the road rises to an overpass take the dead-end road to the right. Seattle Rendering Works is at the end of the long, narrow road.*

The Port of Seattle has yielded to the City of Seattle's insistence that public accesses be provided on the Duwamish Waterways to its working waterfront, a very different thing from a play waterfront. The eateries and gewgaw shops and toy streetcars along Alaskan Way entertain tourists but are no substitute for the ocean-going ships that used to berth on Elliott Bay. The choicest of the half-dozen viewpoints is Terminal 107, close by what's left of Kellogg Island. The island partially spared by the Port as a wildlife refuge was a Duwamish village from approximately 1300 B.P. to the nineteenth-century Holocaust.

Beginning in 1913, the river was straightened, channelized, and dredged, becoming a pair of "waterways" bracketing Harbor Island. At 6 air miles from Elliott Bay it was allowed to retain status as a river, meanders and all. Allentown Bridge gives a look down to olive-green water. (Keep the color in mind for comparison to the progressively less opaque shades upstream.) The Allentown Pea Patch remembers the years not long gone when the Valley alluvium was Seattle's kitchen garden. Railroad tracks permit bicycle-free walking the nearly 2 miles beside the Old Duwamish from the Seattle Rendering Works past the Foster Golf Links to Black River Junction, as the railroad sign says, puzzling newcomers who look in vain for such a river.

BLACK RIVER

Map: 27

Howard Hanson Dam holds back mountain floods from the Green River and dikes keep it in the permitted channel. However, local rainfall can't climb the dikes to get in the river. Without pumping stations the floodplain still would flood. Once you start messing around with Mother Nature there's no end of it.

Directions: *From I-5 south, take Exit 157 over the freeway. Go right at the second light (68 Avenue South, which soon becomes Monster Road SW). King County Pump Station No. 1 is at 550 Monster Road SW, with side-of-the-road parking at the fence.*

King County Pump Station No. 1 provides public parking. A service road follows the ditch in which the Black River flows, when it has any water, to the confluence with the Green—the birthplace of the Duwamish. Let the eye slip into way-back focus. See the Duwamish people paddling or poling dugout canoes on the all-water route from Elliott Bay to Issaquah. See the barges carrying coal from Newcastle, the paddlewheel steamboats bringing garden truck to market. See the young ladies with parasols being paddled or rowed by their swains on Sunday voyages from Georgetown to Renton.

A mowed lane goes from the pump station to a stormwater retention pond. On a day in late June I observed four large families of Canada geese. Ducks quacking. Swallows swooping. Killdeer squealing. Splashings of mysterious creatures diving and surfacing.

On a day in late June I observed four large families of Canada geese. Ducks quacking. Swallows swooping. Killdeer squealing.

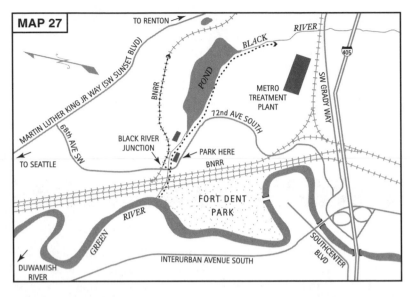

The far shore of the pond was a jungle of tall cottonwoods swaying in the breeze. That this little Black River Riparian Park survived to be given that name is owing to an Auduboner who discovered a great blue heron nesting site, annual rendezvous for a hundred or more birds.

In a scant ½ mile the pond curves south to the mouth of a branch of the Black that ditch-drains the site of the (disappeared) Longacres Race Track. At the far east end of the pond a bayou exits from the forest. Or rather, enters from there, because this is the shrunken remnant of the Black that primevally flowed from Lake Washington.

Across the pond the rails of the Burlington-Northern Railroad can be walked past the heronry forest to heavy industry. The old Seattle & Walla Walla ran a few yards away; the grade can be discerned in the tall grass at forest's edge. Rails first reached the Black River in 1877, when the Seattle & Walla Walla arrived from Georgetown, headed for Renton, and ultimately the Newcastle mines if never Walla Walla. In 1883 the Northern Pacific linked the Black River to Tacoma and Portland and the East. By 1909, when the Milwaukee came through, five lines passed the junction. There still is a north–south mainline and, easterly toward Renton, the former Milwaukee, kept minimally alive by mergerization into the Burlington-Northern.

The high historical excitement, though, comes just beyond the pump station. Spared, doubtless accidentally, from dredging for the retention pond is a cutoff meander, an oxbow marsh. The Black lives!

Green River near Isaac Evans Park

"RIVER OF GREEN"
Maps: 28A, 28B, 29, 30A, 30B, 31

The poetics of the concept—a trail, or at least a nonmotorized travelway, from Whulge to the Cascade front—stirred my feet. I walked most of the way, examined the rest from riverbank roads, and wrote it all up in an earlier edition of this book. However, further reflection brought me to the conclusion that (1) most of the walking there interests only the neighbors, and they don't need no gollydang guidebook to their backyard, and (2) the primary use is bikeway, and bless it for that, but for much walking, no thanks.

Nevertheless, the Big Valley is so awesome a work of the Canadian glacier, and so recent, that pedestrians ought to come for a look. Following are several suggested walk-and-looks:

Tukwila (map 28A). In the 2½ miles from I-405 to the south city limits the Green is channelized and diked and fully domesticated by Southcenter. The riverside paths of Bicentennial and Christiansen Greenbelt Parks swarm.

Kent (maps 28B, 29, 30A, 30B). Russell Road Park has ample room for a cityful of picnickers plus soccer riots of European violence plus paths in views across the river and valley to Issaquah Alps, Beacon Hill, and Rainier. Part of the Green River Natural Resource Area,

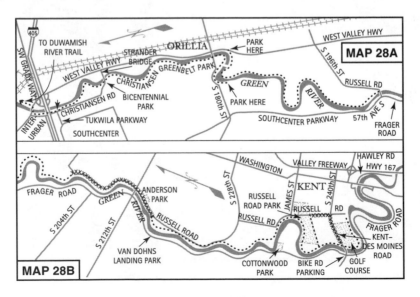

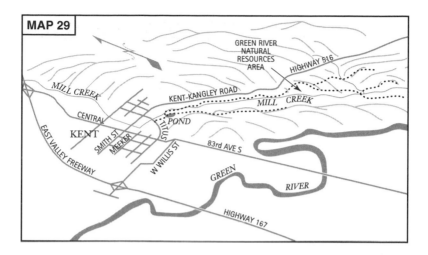

Mill Creek Canyon Park occupies 100 acres of a green gash in the Big Valley wall; from the east edge of the city, trails ascend 2 miles through canyon forest, "wildness within."

Auburn (maps 30A, 30B). From downtown Kent the Green River Road runs 4-odd miles through North Green River Park, meanders and gravel bars, to Isaac Evans Park, connected to Henry Dykstra Park by a swinging footbridge that sets little children to shrieking and their mothers to screaming.

Green River Community College (maps 30B, 31). Atop the promontory jutting out between the junction of the river and Big Soos Creek lies the 300-acre campus. To get there, drive Highway 18 east from Auburn and shortly after crossing the Green River turn left and follow signs to the main campus entrance, elevation 425 feet. The Department of Forestry has a curriculum in forest management that includes tending some 4 miles of trails. These sample big-tree wildlands on the plateau, forests on the steep bluffs, and tanglewoods of birdland sloughs along the Green River, elevation 75 feet. From the street bounding the east edge of campus, five or so trailheads lead into the woods, this way, that way, around and around.

Green Valley. The Green River doesn't really feel at home in the 2-mile-wide vastness where the glacier's Big River flowed. It "belongs" in its own homey little valley, the floodplain at most ½ mile wide, extending downstream 7 miles from the Green River Gorge. Due to lack of communication among transportation engineers who knew nothing about feet and horses, and hikers/horsers who knew plenty but weren't

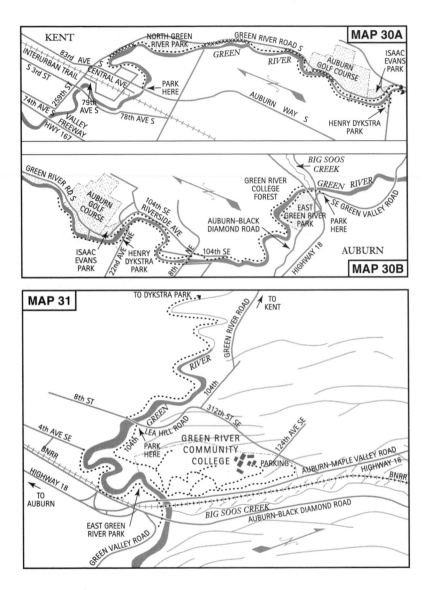

asked, and farmers appalled by learning that their fields were to be a wheel-clogged freeway/bikeway, the planned nonmotorized travelway through the valley sank without a trace in 1993. However, a parallel grand vision, the Farmlands Preservation Program, saved 926 acres.

So, for now, be content to drive through *not* in haste. Go slow, to converse with the cows and horses. Keep the window open; in early

summer the entire valley reeks of strawberries, in fall of corn. Real strawberries, real corn, not the watery synthetics fabricated in California.

Hark! What is this odd aural sensation? A person newly arrived
from the rackety-bang of the Big Valley believes his/her ears have cut
out. It is the sound of—no, not silence, but *quiet*. The green valley walls
make no sound, nor do the green fields. Cars pass on the valley road
only occasionally, muted by so much greenery. As many as a dozen minutes may pass without the brain being jellied by a jet. It is eerie to be
able to hear faraway dogs barking.

GREEN RIVER GORGE

Upon issuing from the Cascade front, the Green River enters a canyon
whose walls rise as much as 300 feet, always steep and often vertical, even
overhanging. For 6 air miles, or 12 stream miles, its meanders are entrenched in solid rock, slicing through some 9000 feet of tilted strata of
shale and sandstone, coal seams interbedded and fossil imprints imbed-
ded of shells and vegetation.

There is absolutely nothing in the region that compares. (There
used to be on the Nisqually and Cowlitz, but those canyons were
drowned by Tacoma City Light.) From the time the coal miners arrived, a century and odd decades ago, the gorge has been a scenic
attraction. In the mid-1960s, Wolf Bauer undertook a detailed survey
of the gorge on foot and in kayak and drew up a proposal for "a unique
natural showcase of free-flowing wild river and primeval canyon." The
legislature was converted by his lobbying and established the Green
River Gorge Conservation Area, appointing as administrating agency
Washington State Parks, charged with acquiring the gorge, rim to
rim, entry to exit.

Hampered by the intermittent bounty of the legislature and the
desultory enthusiasm of upper
management, State Parks has pur-
sued the Bauer Plan at such a pace
that his grail may be finally
achieved in this millennium. I am
unable to provide definite information because the upper management does not answer my letters

> *The Green River enters a
> canyon whose walls rise as
> much as 300 feet, always
> steep and often vertical, even
> overhanging.*

or take my phone calls. (Was it something I said?) Much of the area along the river from Green Valley to the closed-to-the-public watershed of Tacoma City Water is in ownership of the state, which in addition has easements through private property. However, except for the pair of state parks at the gorge's entry and exit, the only clues to state ownership are the neat and tidy white gates that exclude public vehicles (though not feet) from abandoned roads and railroad grades. In a previous edition of this book I described these "white gate" trails, but herein leave them to the pleasure of the guideless explorer.

FLAMING GEYSER STATE PARK

Perimeter loop: 3 miles
High point: 425 feet
Elevation gain: 200 feet
Map: 32

Directions: *East of Auburn, just before Highway 18 crosses the Green River, exit onto Auburn–Black Diamond Road and from that almost immediately exit right onto Green Valley Road. Drive 7 miles east to a Y and go right to the bridge over the river to the park. (Or, stay on the Auburn–Black Diamond Road to the Black Diamond–Enumclaw Road, follow it to 1 mile south of Black Diamond, turn west at the "Flaming Geyser" sign, and drive a scant 3 miles past the Lonely Red Schoolhouse of old Kummer to the bridge.)*

Park at the entry gate to start the loop or, as described here, drive 1¼ miles more to the picnic area parking area, elevation 225 feet. Walk upriver past a series of concrete fish ponds. At the fence corner, turn right up Christy Creek. (Side trip: Cross the creek to a Y, take the right, then the left, gaining 100 feet above the river, dropping to a sandy flat, and ending at the mouth of the gorge. Snoop around the corner of a cliff of stratified rock.)

Pass a pool bubbling gas, the flow from a pipe ignited (sometimes) to form a flame 6 to 12 inches high. In 1911 a test hole probing coal seams was drilled 1403 feet down. At 900 to 1000 feet were showings of methane gas. In early days of the former private resort, the "Geyser" was flaming many feet in the air; now it's pretty well pooped out.

Follow the riverbank upstream to the picnic area, by sandy beaches, through patches of woods, meeting ducks and dippers, gulls and herons.

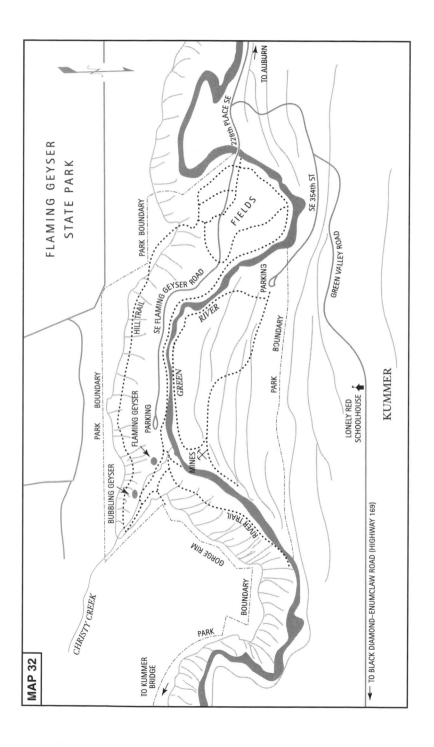

MAP 32

FLAMING GEYSER
STATE PARK

N

CHRISTY CREEK

TO KUMMER
BRIDGE

PARK BOUNDARY

GORGE RIM

RIVER TRAIL

BUBBLING GEYSER

PARK BOUNDARY

HILL TRAIL

FLAMING GEYSER
PARKING

MINES

SE FLAMING GEYSER ROAD

GREEN RIVER

PARK BOUNDARY

FIELDS

PARKING

228th PLACE SE

SE 354th ST

TO AUBURN

GREEN VALLEY ROAD

LONELY RED
SCHOOLHOUSE

KUMMER

TO BLACK DIAMOND–ENUMCLAW ROAD (HIGHWAY 169)

Green River from Flaming Geyser State Park

Continue over a bridge and up the creek in mossy-ferny maple woods, the trail dividing and uniting, passing a bridge and stub trail to the gray mud of Bubbling Geyser. Up a short set of stairs and then again upstream, the main trail recrosses the creek and ascends the bluff, topping out at 425 feet, and begins a long upsy-downsy contour along the sidehill in a green tangle of maple and cedar and alder and lichen and moss. The way at length drops to the floodplain and road, the trail now a mowed strip (or strips) in pasture grass. Cross the road

Kayaking in Green River Gorge

and walk out in the field to the park-entry bridge. Turn right and follow the riverbank upstream to the picnic area, by sandy beaches, through patches of woods, meeting ducks and dippers, gulls and herons, and kayakers landing after voyages down the gorge.

KUMMER (BLACK DIAMOND) BRIDGE
Map: 33A

Directions: *Drive Highway 169 south 2½ miles from Black Diamond.*

The view of the gorge the best known to the most people is from the walkway of this bridge. Giddy gazing into the vasty deeps.

From the parking area on the north side of the bridge, elevation 450 feet, several paths dive to the river. Fishermen! A person managing to arrive intact at the river finds paths downstream about ½ mile and upstream a short way to a handsome sandstone cliff. In low water the walk can be extended indefinitely in both directions. On the south side of the bridge a plummet leads to upstream–downstream boulder-hopping.

GREEN RIVER GORGE RESORT
Maps: 33A, 33B

Directions: *From Highway 169 in Black Diamond, turn east on Green River Gorge Road 4 miles to the Franklin Bridge. (Alternatively, from Highway 169 at 1.5 miles south of the Kummer Bridge, take the Enumclaw-Franklin Road 4 miles to the Franklin Bridge.) Park near the inn, elevation 580 feet.*

In the 1920s, the Diamond Stage Company began running Studebaker buses to the Green River Gorge, described in promotional brochures as possessing "a beauty that far surpasses any other scenic attraction in this Charmed Land." Resorts proliferated in the vicinity. Lake Retreat, Lake Sawyer Paradise, Lake 12 ("A delightful family resort—a rest room beneath the stars—a trysting place for man and health"), and Ye Olde Green River Gorge Resort, which was "so crowded on weekends that you barely had room to move," recalls old settler Tom Zumek. "On Sundays we had motorcycle races up the slag pile." There were a Knights of Pythias hall, a baseball field, a saloon (until Prohibition, when bootleggers met the demand, and so pugnaciously that revenooers abstained from visiting the coal country), and a dance pavilion "where bands strained to be heard above the din of the falls."

When the range of automobiles extended beyond the Coal Country to the mountains, the resort declined to a dark and seedy, half-abandoned, often-closed time. In the 1970s a group of new owners entertained themselves brushing out trails, selling a map, operating a snackery. Popularity returned, unfortunately much of it fueled by booze and drugs. The cost of liability insurance forced closure. This being the Quintessential Gorge, it must have a public future. What's holding up State Parks? Aside from legislative stinginess and bureaucratic lethargy? Doubtless the formidable expense of renovation and operation at a time when existing parks are being closed for lack of funds.

For decades the main entry was from the snackery building down

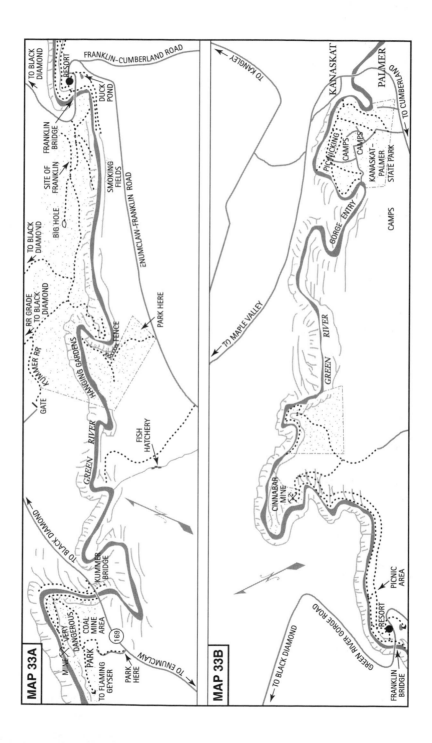

MAP 33A

TO BLACK DIAMOND

RESORT

FRANKLIN-CUMBERLAND ROAD

DUCK POND

FRANKLIN BRIDGE

SITE OF FRANKLIN

SMOKING FIELDS

BIG HOLE

TO BLACK DIAMOND

RR GRADE TO BLACK DIAMOND

ENUMCLAW-FRANKLIN ROAD

PARK HERE

KUMMER RR

GATE

FENCE

HANGING GARDENS

GREEN RIVER

FISH HATCHERY

TO BLACK DIAMOND

KUMMER BRIDGE

MINE - VERY DANGEROUS

COAL MINE AREA

PARK

169

TO ENUMCLAW

TO FLAMING GEYSER

PARK HERE

MAP 33B

TO KANGLEY

KANASKAT

PALMER

TO CUMBERLAND

PICNICKING CAMPS

CAMPS

KANASKAT-PALMER STATE PARK

GORGE ENTRY

CAMPS

TO MAPLE VALLEY

GREEN RIVER

CINNABAR MINE

TO BLACK DIAMOND

GREEN RIVER GORGE ROAD

FRANKLIN BRIDGE

RESORT

PICNIC AREA

Green River Gorge Resort

to a **Y**. The left heads downstream on a staircase-path over the brink of a waterfall to the river—dark clefts between huge mossy-green boulders, slippery slabs beside churning green pools of The Chute, under fern-and-moss cliffs and Rainbow Falls.

The right from the **Y** goes upstream ¼ mile and descends a staircase to a forest flat by the river. This is a loop trail—but only at low water because at high water a stretch of several hundred feet requires knee-deep wading. For seasons when the trail is submerged, a straight-up path climbs to the gorge rim. The other end of the loop trail descends spectacularly on staircases to the river and a **T**. The left fork goes downstream (the loop way) to a high-water end at a wonderful cave. The right fork, a delight every step, proceeds to exposed coal seams.

FRANKLIN BRIDGE

Maps: 33A, 33B

In the late 1880s an impressive engineering feat emplaced a wooden span over the Quintessential Gorge to link Black Diamond to Cumberland, Bayne, and Palmer. In 1915 it was replaced by a Baltimore Petit truss, the sole example of that design in King County. Closed for repairs in 1987, it reopened in 1991. The walk-across views to the gorge depths shiver the imaginations of gazers recalling the bridge's past as the region's favorite Lover's Leap.

The hamlet of Franklin lay across the river from the resort building. A white gate bars the entry from the Green River Gorge Road, elevation 608 feet.

What tales I could tell of walking 3 miles on the old railroad grade from the site of old Franklin town to Black Diamond! But I won't. (Get to a library and look up the previous edition of this book.)

BLACK DIAMOND MUSEUM

Before software and latte, before aircraft, before timber, fish, and Alaska, King Coal ruled King County. Axis of the industry was the railroad from the coal dock on Elliott Bay, up the Duwamish to Black River Junction, a branch to Newcastle, the main line through Maple Valley to Black Diamond, Kummer, Franklin, Cumberland, Durham, Hyde, Bayne, Palmer, and the rest. In 1880 the Black Diamond

Black Diamond Museum

Mining Company of Nortonville, California, discovered the McKay Seam, the highest-quality coal ever found on the Pacific Coast, and in 1884 the rails reached the new town of Black Diamond, which in a year grew from a tent village to a population of 3000 and by the turn of the century 3500, the biggest producer of coal in the county. In the 1920s petroleum elbowed coal off the throne. The old Pacific Coast Coal Company shriveled. In 1933 the Palmer Coking Coal Company bought up much of its property and in the 1980s, through a subsidiary nostalgically reviving the name of Pacific Coast Coal, opened the John Henry, an enormous open pit.

Historical societies thrive in Issaquah, Newcastle, Renton, and Maple Valley, as well as Black Diamond. In 1976 the last-named society, its founding occasioned by the nation's bicentennial, undertook restoration of the railroad depot, abandoned for that purpose since the 1930s. In 1982 the museum opened.

Society members who took time from their refurbishments of the jail, wash house, "model mine" with mine cars and electric locomotive, told me tales of the "bump" that killed miners in the mile-deep No. 11 Seam, of the strike in 1921 when locked-out miners moved a short way west to found Morganville, named for the hospitable farmer who let them squat on his land, and of the product which gave Black Diamond a new fame in Prohibition, not necessarily because it was so much better than could be obtained in Seattle, but because it was sold so openly, lawmen knowing better than to mess with these miners.

KANASKAT–PALMER STATE PARK

Two sample loops: total 3½ miles
High point: 740 feet
Elevation gain: none
Map: 33B

Directions: *Drive via Enumclaw or Black Diamond to old Cumberland and thence to old Palmer. Alternatively, drive from Issaquah-Landsburg or Kent to old Georgetown (that is, the Ravensdale Market). Turn east 1 mile on Kent-Kangley Road to a Y. Keep right on Retreat-Kangley Road 3 miles and turn right on Cumberland-Kanaskat Road. Proceed 1.7 miles, passing through old Kanaskat and crossing the Green River to old Palmer and the entry to Kanaskat–Palmer State Park.*

Trails take off from a number of points on the park's road system, and all are excellent woods walks, lending themselves to any number of loops. For the best, at a Y in 0.6 mile at the park entrance, keep left. In 0.2 mile more pass a side road left. In a final 0.2 mile is the turn-around at the picnic area. Elevation, 740 feet.

A path leads upstream 1 long mile to intersect the entry road. A dead-end path starts at the turnaround circle and drops to a gravel bar. Just upstream, the river falls over sandstone slabs into a spacious swimming pool.

The major trail downstream diverges from this dead-end path and passes a privy, a picnic shelter in a broad lawn, and dozens of picnic sites tucked into a forest new-growing after a semi–clear-cut in 1976. At the end of the picnic area the blacktop trail veers left to the

Just upstream, the river falls over sandstone slabs into a spacious swimming pool.

entry road; the river trail enters mixed forest. Rude side paths demand side trips to choice spots to sit beside the river. In ¾ mile the trail ends. Walk out onto sandstone slabs beveled flat at the base of sandstone cliffs—not high, but announcing what lies just ahead. Stand at the edge of the beveled slab and look down into the water. E-gad! Retreat! The bottom can barely be made out, perhaps 12 feet down. Gaze upstream to a jut of rock, and downstream, where the beginnings of the gorge can be guessed just around the horseshoe bend.

NOLTE STATE PARK (DEEP LAKE)

Lake circuit and side trips: 1½ miles
High point: 770 feet
Elevation gain: none

Directions: *From Cumberland, drive south 1 mile to the park, elevation 770 feet.*

The park is officially closed September to April, but the trail is always open to feet.

Not in the gorge but near it is 39-acre Deep Lake, owned by the Nolte family since 1883, operated as a private resort since 1913, and in the late 1960s willed to the public by Minnie Nolte. During olden-day logging only the cream (the huge cedars) was skimmed; the forest of Douglas firs up to 6 feet in diameter appears virginal, fit companion for the quiet (no motorboats) water.

The trail loops 1 mile around the lake, heads through the big firs and 5-foot cedars and 3-foot cottonwoods, crosses the inlet, Deep Creek, and passes a number of birding paths to the shore.

MOUNT McDONALD

Round trip: 8 miles
High point: 3280 feet
Elevation gain: 2400 feet
Map: 34

A splendid snowline-prober, when wheels are frozen out, through a succession of chapters in the geography of Whulge country. From the Cascade front between the valleys of the Cedar and Green Rivers, look across the upland sliced by the Green River Gorge to the Osceola Mudflow and The Mountain from which it gushed. Look to the peninsula thrust of the Issaquah Alps touching shores of Lake Washington. See Seattle and the Olympics and the steam plume rising from the Tacoma pall.

Directions: *The trailhead can be driven to by any number of routes, all easy to find and confusing to describe. Use a road map. At 0.7 mile past a Bonneville switch station on the Kanaskat-Kangley Road, spot a narrow lane on the east, SE Courtney Road, elevation 874 feet. Park on the highway shoulder, not up the lane.*

Walk up Courtney Road a short bit through the barking dogs. Cross the rail grade, which had tracks until the late 1970s. Turn left on a woods road to a gate. Climb steadily in mixed forest, spurs going off left and right. In ½ mile a window opens to pastures below and out to the Olympics and Rainier. At 1 mile is a waterfall-creek. As the road twists and turns around the mountain, the forest changes to young conifers, mostly hemlocks, and views commence over treetops and through them. At 3 miles, 2828 feet, is a Y where both forks are major. Go right, climbing. The views on this trip are cafeteria-like—something of this here, a bit of that there, never everything at once. In this stretch are the best views north, down to the Cedar River and out to Taylor and Tiger and Squak and Cougar, as well as to Rattlesnake and Si, Baker and Index and Three Fingers.

In a final 1 mile, with a couple more switchbacks, the road passes a dead end right to a gravel pit, stays left to a gate, and in a final ⅓

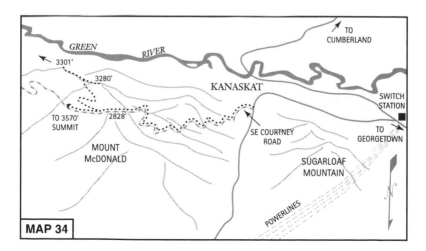

MAP 34

Mount Rainier from Mount McDonald

mile tops out on a clear-cut plateau atop McDonald Point, elevation 3280 feet. Here, formerly the site of a fire lookout, is a TV repeater. Enjoy the grand view off the edge of the scarp. Then, for a variation, follow a sketchy road ¼ mile through small silver firs and western hemlocks to a 3301-foot point. See huge Rainier and nearby Grass. See the Enumclaw plain and silvery meanders of the Green River and hear the trains blow, boys, hear the trains blow.

SOOS CREEK (GARY GRANT) PARK

Round trip: from Lake Meridian Park to SE 208 Street 8¾ miles
High point: 450 feet
Elevation gain: 50 feet
Map: 35

Big Soos Creek is an example of the "undersized" stream, not big enough for its inherited britches. The valley it follows was dug by a far mightier flow of water, gone these dozen millennia. Gravels of braided channels that once swung from valley wall to valley wall have

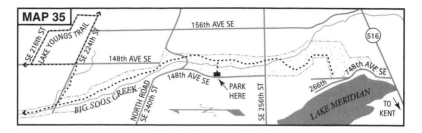

been buried by peat bogs, cattail marshes, willow swamps. The usual fate of undersized creeks is to be filled, water ditched or sewered, houses and shopping center built. The Forward Thrust of the 1960s saved a long strip of Big Soos from such a fate—5 air miles, up to ¼ mile wide. In the late 1980s King County Parks began building an end-to-end trail, a blacktop lane for bicycles and wheelchairs, a dirt lane for horses, walkers welcome to both.

The good news: a sidehill forest of tall firs, a bottom woodland of willows, a striking bridge over the creek by a children-friendly wading pool, pastoral vistas, ponds dredged to retain stormwater and nourish cattails, blackbirds harassing walkers, and salmon fry leaping for mosquitoes. When complete, a 10-mile round trip of good news.

The bad news: King County Parks waited too long, houses got built, a public trail is not welcome in front yards and not ecologically tolerable or legal in the wetlands alternative. The walker from afar is advised to be content with an 8-mile round trip.

Directions: *Drive Highway 516 to Lake Meridian Park. Turn north on 148 Avenue SE 0.4 mile to 266th. Though the park continues south to Lake Meridian, the 266th trailhead is calmer. Elevation, 400 feet.*

OTHER TRIPS

Lake Youngs Perimeter Trail. The fourth-largest lake in lowland King County has no swimming beaches, no hydroplane races, and, as the holding reservoir between the Cedar River and Seattle City Water mains, is rarely seen by the public, though sipped and swallowed by it daily. Forests cover three-quarters of the 4 square miles of the reservation. A 9-mile King County Parks trail on a Seattle Water Department 25-foot-wide dedication follows the fence.

Big Soos Railroad Trail. From the rail bridge over the Green River, the living rails and ties give 4 miles of wild woodland walking up the Big Soos valley, in a secluded ravine to the start of farms at the confluence with Jenkins Creek.

Opposite: *White River from Game Farm Wilderness Park*

WHITE RIVER

WHITE RIVER

Management: Auburn Parks, State Parks, U.S. Forest Service, Weyerhaeuser
Topographic maps: Lake Tapps, Auburn, Sumner, Buckley, Enumclaw, Cumberland, Greenwater, Lester—and their equivalents in the Green Trails series, privately published

Northernmost of Rainier's great rivers. The shortest route from Puget Sound City to the national park. The closest The Mountain comes to The Whulge.

Elevations mostly so high that snowline-probing is the prime sport. Comparatively little country low enough for year-around walking.

Black sands, black and red boulders. That's lava rock. There's a volcano upstream. Murky water, a wide bed of channels old and new. That's rock milk and channel-braiding. There's a glacier upstream. A dangerous combination, a glacier and a volcano.

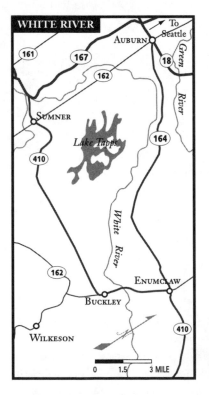

Tell it to the Original Inhabitants who were going about their business 5800 years ago when the steam bomb exploded 3 miles away, melting thousands of tons of snow and ice, sending down the valley to Whulge a roaring slurry of muck, perhaps 2.5 billion cubic yards of it, three-quarters of a cubic mile of rock debris. The Osceola Mudflow. Leaving in the lowlands a deposit up to 70 feet thick. A once-in-a-dozen-millennia rarity? No. The Mountain has spewed sixty such "lahars" in the last 10,000 years. At least one dumped icewater and rubbish in Elliott Bay and Lake Washington. Just 600 years ago the Electron Mudflow rumbled down the Puyallup to saltwater. Come the next big show and real estate in Enumclaw, Buckley, Kent, Auburn, Sumner, and Puyallup—all of whose sites were buried by the Osceola—won't be worth a nickel. A scientific study published in 1994 warned, "A major volcanic eruption or debris flow could kill thousands of residents and cripple the economy of the Pacific Northwest."

If man has performed no single so dramatic a stunt of river manipulation, he's puttered for decades, tinkering this way and that with the White. The diking by King County farmers to transfer flooding problems to Pierce County farmers led in 1914 to an agreement for joint management and cost-sharing.

A disastrous flood of the 1930s couldn't be blamed on anybody but Nature, whose ever-doughty foes, the Army engineers, answered the bugle call by heaping up the Mud Mountain Dam; the river is no longer permitted to flood and in flood season often is reservoirized by the dam, whose fate in the next Osceola amuses Luddites.

Last, in 1911 Puget Power put the White to work, at Buckley diverting water through a flume to a reservoir, Lake Tapps, thence into turbines at Deiringer and a return to the White (Stuck) in the Big Valley. The White thus is a tamed river. But it doesn't feel tame. The hiker keeps an ear cocked, alert for dull distant booms up thataway.

GAME FARM WILDERNESS PARK

Round trip: 1–6–10 miles
High point: 100–500 feet
Elevation gain: 0–400 feet
Map: 36

Downstream, the Stuck River flows south through the Big Valley in a tidily diked channel between rows of houses and fields of cows. Upstream the White River issues from a wildland where braided channels migrate back and forth across a floodplain/floodway between tanglewood walls. Here, several minutes' walk from a Metro bus stop, a person might be in Mount Rainier National Park.

Directions: *From Auburn, drive south on Auburn Way toward Buckley. Exit on R Street and continue about 1 mile to the bridge over the Stuck-White River. Turn left at the park sign to the entrance, elevation 100 feet.*

Though the Auburn city park is not quite ½ mile long, before there was a park I walked the dike 3 miles, until school bells rang, warning that the motorcycle hoodlums were being let out of their daytime detention center. (Fences and rangers now exclude them.) The river is, of course, the best walking route, on bars of black sand and boulders of black andesite and red andesite. Exactly as in the national park, the walker feels close to volcano and glaciers, the Osceola Mudflow.

The river flow at any given hour is determined by how much water Puget Power is diverting into Lake (Reservoir) Tapps to serve the Deiringer powerhouse. Often the river has barely enough water to float the fish, as the State Fisheries folks are wont to complain. But one sunny day in 1976 the river was turned on full flow without notice and two children were drowned in their front yard. Keep in mind the possibilities of unannounced "walls of water."

The route upstream soon leaves the wide-open spaces of the Big Valley for the cloistered White Valley. Ducks swim, fish jump, kingfishers dive. In low water (when the glaciers aren't melting and all the TV sets are turned on), the river is a safe and easy wade from side to side, back and forth. Follow a bar until it pinches out, wade a channel to another bar. Above the Puget Power diversion intake you'll have to cut that out, of course, but by then you're almost to Mud Mountain Dam.

The "Game Farm" of the name derives from the pens where the State Game Department raised shotgun targets until the site was taken over for Auburn playfields. Dikes on that side of the river are a popular Sunday stroll and a good jump-off for river-walkers. Calling the park "Wilderness" seems cheeky until a person has gone adventuring upstream.

One would never guess, driving through farms on the plain of the Osceola Mudflow, that a stone's throw distant, down the 125–250-foot bluffs, is a river bottom where the human presence is virtually unfelt. Old and very old woods roads wander this way and that, and fishermen's paths seek riverbanks, and gypos cut alder and river-rafted cedar logs, and here and there are glimpses of houses on the brink of the bluff. But

Calling the park "wilderness" seems cheeky until a person has gone adventuring upstream.

most of the time, down there in the broad bottom up to 1 mile wide, amid braided, shifting channels, marshy sloughs, tanglewoods, and beaver ponds, one could imagine the year to be 1850—or 1650.

In 1977 I found a woods road descending to the river and walked and waded 5 miles downstream, wondering if I'd somehow missed Auburn and might soon meet Dr. Livingston. Not so cheeky after all.

MOUNT PETE

Round trip: 2½ miles
High point: 1801 feet
Elevation gain: 1031 feet
Map: 37

Highest of the mountainlets that pimple the pastured plain, Pete is the monarch of the Enumclaw Blobs. How come they are? The Canadian glacier sculpted their basalt into hard hearts of steepness. The Osceola Mudflow gushed out from the mountain front and surrounded them with flatness. How come the chief pimple survived as a grand stand of virgin forest, a wildland arboretum? Well, in 1979 the state Department of Natural Resources proposed to log part of it, and one would have thought the proposal was to install Golden Arches in the Garden of Eden. Somebody loves ol' Pete.

Pete? Most of the local population just moved in from Iowa only last week. They never have heard of the private park founded by Pete, a hero for building a civic swimming pool, and they have tin ears. They

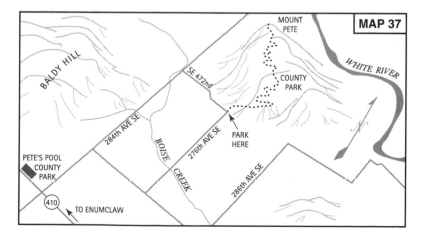

Columnar basalt on Mount Pete

think the peak that stands high above the pool is "Mount Peak." As in, say, "Lake Water." A humorless geographer couldn't handle the local patois and installed "Pinnacle Peak" on government maps. Until the mid-1960s, when we began publishing guidebooks, the only non-locals who ever walked to the top were Mountaineers. They knew Pete. So for us and all other people who know where they are, it's Pete, and never mind those talking heads on the TV; in a little while they'll be off to LA or SF or back to Iowa.

Directions: *Drive Highway 410 to the eastern outskirts of Enumclaw, and at the Enumclaw Park swimming pool (formerly Pete's Pool) turn south on 284 Avenue SE. Follow it 1.5 miles and turn west (right) on SE 472. In 0.5 mile, at a sharp bend right, park on the shoulder by the obvious trailhead, elevation 770 feet.*

The 1-mile trail is very steep and can be slippery but is wide and well beaten. Beginning in lush undergrowth of a moist, mixed forest displaying at least four species of ferns and lots of frogs, the way quickly ascends to startling big Douglas firs, up to 4 feet thick, plus a full assortment of other good green things suitable for a virgin forest. In ¾ mile the path joins the old road built to serve the lookout tower, removed in the mid-1960s. In ¼ mile the road-trail, after passing the finest of many displays of columnar basalt, curves around to an end close under the summit, 1801 feet.

Beginning in lush undergrowth of a moist, mixed forest displaying at least four species of ferns and lots of frogs, the way quickly ascends to startling big Douglas firs.

With the tower gone and the trees a-growing, the panorama ain't the 360-degree circle of yore. It would not be criminally sacrilegious to open windows to beautiful downtown Enumclaw and other points west, to vistas from the Issaquah Alps to McDonald, Boise Ridge, Grass—and Rainier, the Clearwater River valley and Three Sisters prominent. In mind's eye one can see the Osceola Mudflow surging down the White River valley, dividing to sweep around both sides of Pete and overwhelm villages of The People. (Is the racial memory responsible for the name, "Enumclaw," which means "place of the evil spirits"?)

THREE SISTERS

Map: 38

Hikers driving toward virgin forests and flower meadows and dazzling glaciers of Mount Rainier may not notice, just as they leave the lowlands, a huge mass of landscape lofting steeply above the White River. If they do, they may wish it weren't there, so they could see The Mountain. What they don't realize is that this is The Mountain, the outermost bulwark.

Surveying for the *Footsore* series, I sampled the stump-farm road-trails from the Bridge Creek Gate entry (now a tollgate) to Weyerhaeuser's ill-gotten empire. I even drove the 18.3 miles (then tollfree) to within an hour's stroll of 4980-foot Three Sisters 1, "Old Snagtop," where a runaway slash fire killed the summit trees, which were anyway too spindly to be worth hauling to the mill.

In the 1970s the supervisor of Mt. Baker–Snoqualmie National Forest, Don Campbell, felt the mixed federal–private lands northwest of the national park were being overlooked as a recreational resource. In 1978 I submitted to him, on request, a proposal that the

Forest Service exchange some lands and acquire some easements for a trail corridor from a Metro bus stop in Buckley up South Prairie Creek, whose slot canyons of tumbling cataracts and ancient firs were literally wilder than the interior of the North Cascades. Don praised my report as the sort of imaginative thinking needed to complement and extend traditional programs of park enlargement and wilderness establishment. I had real hope that Greater Mount Rainier would be connected by trail to a bus stop—"National Park on the Metro"—but on my next survey I found that logging trucks had discovered those hidden groves of ancient firs, and the canyons were wiped as clean as the ridges. So I wasn't surprised when Don, bless his memory, took early retirement.

The trail is still a possibility. Another possibility was proposed in the previous edition of this book. Again, no takers. A trail could cross Mud Mountain Dam, 1300 feet, hook up Champion and Weyerhaeuser booty lands via old logging roads and bits of new-built trail, and climb

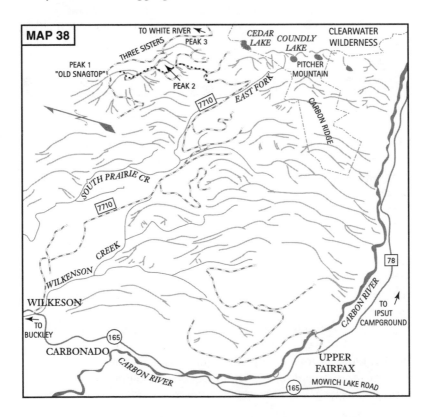

in some 5 miles to the 3969-foot summit of Three Sisters 3, at the tip of the ridge. Airplane-wing views.

In 1978 my nose, aided by flashes of supernatural revelation, puzzled out a route to the summit ridge free from the vagaries (and ultimately, the tolls) of the Weyerhaeuser gate. Starting from Wilkeson, a maze of unsigned logging roads was solved to an end up South Fork, then East Fork South Prairie Creek. The latter was waded to a 1930s logging railroad grade from which a genuine Forest Service trail ascended into an astonishing scrap of virgin forest, emerged at 3800 feet into the awesome devastation of a 1970s clear-cut. Nothing thereafter to obscure the routefinding except stumps, elk paths were followed through the slash to the top of Three Sisters 1, Old Snagtop. Railroad logging ended here in the 1950s, the scalping completed by truck logging. No need in this out-of-the-way corner of The Mountain's ecosystem to fret about public relations; I looked down from the summit, aghast to see chainsaws slaughtering a patch of short but thick-butted and very ancient trees at the edge of a subalpine meadow-marsh. As free-marketeers are wont to chortle, people have consciences but Adam Smith's Invisible Hand doesn't need one; a profit-and-loss sheet handles every venial and mortal sin, as well as the general run of capital crimes.

In 1993 Ira and Pat Spring, searching for the old Forest Service trail to the Clearwater Wilderness loop (see *100 Hikes in the South Cascades and Olympics*) got lost and accidentally retraced, sort of, my 1978 route. My daughter Penny, trying to do the same, was intimidated on her first sortie by hurtling logging trucks but on her second (a Sunday) had better luck.

Nevertheless, I don't know where they're still finding trees to log, and won't attempt to predict where the roads will be, and can pretty well guarantee the signing will be sketchy, and therefore suggest that adventurers come with low expectations, an abundance of maps, and an understanding that timber companies have no shame. Assuming the Force is with you, several miles from the car, on logging roads, bulldozer tracks, and elk-stompings, after an elevation gain of 1500 feet or so, you will stand atop Old Snagtop.

Beyond the millions of stumps on private lands are more of the same on Forest Service multiple-use lands, and then the Clearwater Wilderness and Mount Rainier National Park. The tree "farm" (never to produce, up here, a second commercial "crop") contrasts shockingly with the virgin green of Carbon Ridge, the dazzling white of The

Mountain's Winthrop Glacier, Little Tahoma, Curtis, and Liberty Ridges and Willis Wall, Ptarmigan Ridge and Echo and Observation, Mowich Face and Sunset Ridge. South over Carbon and Puyallup and Nisqually valleys, Spar Pole Hill and The Divide and Bald Hills and Black Hills. North over the White valley, Boise Ridge–Grass Mountain–Huckleberry Mountain–Dalles Ridge and high Cascades beyond, from Stuart to Chimney to Glacier to Baker. West, Tacoma and Seattle, Whulge and Olympics. The circuits overload. The brain explodes.

GRASS MOUNTAIN

Round trip: anywhere from 6 or so to 17 miles
High point: anywhere from 2500 to 4382 feet
Elevation gain: 1000 to 3000 feet
Map: 39

Grass Mountain is some 15 miles long, rising from the Green River at the Cascade front and extending far into the range, for most of its length forming the north side of the White River valley. The only reason it's not longer is that at a certain point, for no apparent reason, the map gets tired of Grass and starts calling the ridge Huckleberry Mountain. This much mountain obviously provides material for any number of hikes, mostly in the stark landscapes of recent clearcutting, the views beginning early and growing and growing as elevation is gained.

In the late 1970s, while attempting an exhaustive inventory of good lowland walking in and around Puget Sound City, I saw to my anguish and fury how little of Mount Rainier is in its national park, and why an especially hot spot in Dante's Inferno ought to be reserved for the robber barons who so wickedly abused their ill-gotten forest lands. While adventuring on VW beetle and foot through the Weyerhaeuser stumplands, I developed a sort of obscene esthetic taste for these landscapes of Hell. Fortunately for the sake of my soul, the bottom-liner gnomes of Federal Way found still another way to profit from their crime by keeping their entry gates closed tight except a few at which the likes of me (and also the gunners with their meatwagons) would be permitted to pass by payment of a toll. Gratefully I abandoned the entire House of Weyerhaeuser. Except one route, where the never-open gate is a blessing that excludes the panzers, preserves the peace.

Because the way is open to feet at any time of week or year, it can

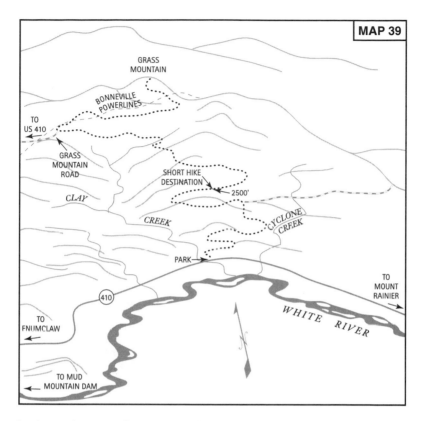

be done when you please. A snowline-prober unmarred by snowplaying 4x4s is a splendid notion, climbing until the kids have thrown all the snowballs they want and the dogs have filled up on white candy and the snow becomes more nuisance than pleasure. Choose a delicious meltwater torrent or an especially big viewpoint and call it a lunch.

Directions: *Drive Highway 410 east 5.9 miles from the turnoff to Mud Mountain Dam. Turn left on the Clay Creek road to a gate always closed to public vehicles. Elevation, 1500 feet.*

The narrow, rough, steep road ascends Clay Creek valley, at ¾ mile, 1900 feet, swinging under a basalt cliff to splendid views of Rainier. (Have the kids thrown enough snowballs yet?) In second-growth from the 1930s, and/or third-growth from the 1990s, the way proceeds on flat railroad grades of lokie days, reused for logging trucks. Excessively exact detailing of the route would overly complicate the routefinding, which in "working" forests is always subject to change without notice. To generalize, the road-trail contours east 1 mile or so to the edge of

Grass Mountain engulfed in clouds

Cyclone Creek valley, then at 2300 feet or so contours west 1 mile or so, then east ½ mile or so to a series of view windows at 2500 feet or so, about 3 miles from the highway. (Far enough?)

Climb until the kids have thrown all the snowballs they want and the dogs have filled up on white candy and the snow becomes more nuisance than pleasure.

For a time the views get no better—rather, worse, as the slope lays back. But the top of the world awaits the long legs. Past the windows, switchback west to a T at 2650 feet. Take the left, on and on over a series of creeklets, each with its ghosts of old trestles, now disappearing in young alder. Windows open on Rainier and up to the scalped summit ridge of Grass. Approaching a Bonneville powerline, which crosses over Grass from Green to the White, and passing a gravel pit, at 6½ miles, 3100 feet, meet the Grass Mountain Road, which comes up from Highway 410 but is gated against public vehicles.

Turn right on this wider road and settle down to grind out altitude. During the first ½ mile, keep right at two Ys; from then on simply forge ahead, passing many obviously dead-ending spurs. The road starts up across the steep final slopes of the mountain, clearcut in the 1960s. Views become overwhelming. At 4000 feet is a saddle; now there are views down to the Lynn Lake basin and north to the Green River. The road ascends the ridge crest on top of the stripped-naked world, to the summit at 4382 feet, 8½ miles.

What a world! Out the White River to Enumclaw, Whulge, Seattle, the Olympics. Across the Green River to McDonald, Issaquah Alps, Si, Baker, Glacier, and beyond the Cascade Crest to Stuart. Let's see, there must be something else. Oh yes, The Mountain.

FEDERATION FOREST STATE PARK 👢

Round trip: 1–9 miles
High point: 1650 feet
Elevation gain: none
Map: 40

Directions: *Drive Highway 410 east from Enumclaw 17 miles to the interpretive center parking area, elevation 1650 feet.*

The twentieth century was only just getting up a full head of steam when the Washington State Federation of Women's Clubs realized there eventually would be no low-elevation ancient forests except in parks. To let the masses see what they would be missing, a stand of big old trees was acquired beside the Snoqualmie Pass Highway east of North Bend. But Weyerhaeuser badly wanted those trees, so handy to its Snoqualmie mill, and warned the women that since the company was clearcutting up to the preserve on all sides, the wind soon would blow down the ancients. The beneficent Bottom Line offered to exchange for a forest in the White River boondocks.

Boondocks no more. A highway has since been built over Cayuse Pass and Chinook Pass. Side-highways lead to the Crystal Mountain Ski Area and Yakima Park in Mount Rainier National Park. Having skinned the White River valley, Weyerhaeuser has turned the stumps over to its Real Estate Division, serving the demi-urge of the "Tree-Eating and Subdivision-Growing Company." The traveler's brain reels as his car carries him out of this "daylight in the swamp" to the 612-acre preserve, the "Land of Giants."

From the interpretive center (open to group tours by appointment only; call 206-663-2207), the two Fred Cleator Interpretive Trails, both loops, the West Trail a scant 1 mile, the East ½ mile, introduce five distinct forest communities on a broad river terrace perched 30 feet above the present level of the White River. Also preserved is a stretch of the Naches Wagon Road, or old Naches Trail, the route from the east of the Longmire Party in 1853. The nature trails and the plantings around the interpretive center are a

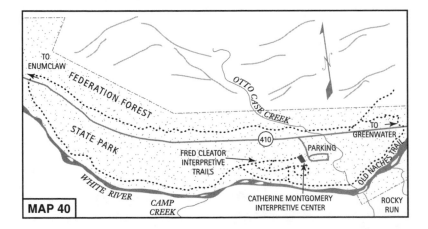

MAP 40

Federation Forest State Park

fine classroom for learning the native shrubs and trees, including ancient Douglas fir, western red cedar, western hemlock, grand fir, and (uncommon this far inland) Sitka spruce.

A 1-mile River Trail takes the feet to gravel bars of the White, which might be followed upstream to the glaciers, downstream to Auburn. The 5-mile loop of the Hobbit Trail tours the park from one end to the other on both sides of the highway. Trees, springs, marshes. The walker surfeited of ogling and gasping at forest giants and ghostly saprophytes can burst free from green twilight and be struck blind by the bright day of the glacier-fed river.

OTHER TRIPS

Baldy Hill. The 1580-foot east summit of Mount Pete's twin (except it has lost all its hair) is attained via a gated logging road in a long 1 mile from the White River Mill.

Mud Mountain Dam. The Vista Trail descends ⅓ mile to dam views. The White River Rim Trail, briefly the most popular low-elevation walk in the area, was obliterated by a Weyerhaeuser clear-cut and not replaced by the Corps of Engineers. But service roads descend to the river, where the reservoir is filled only in flood time, and gravel bars can be walked 5 miles to the terminus of the destroyed Rim Trail at Scatter Creek.

Opposite: *Puyallup River and moon rising over Mount Rainier*

PUYALLUP RIVER

PUYALLUP RIVER

Management: Tacoma Parks, Pierce County Parks, State Parks.
Topographic maps: USGS Lake Tapps, Enumclaw, Wilkeson, Buckley, Orting, Sumner—and their equivalents in the Green Trails series, privately published

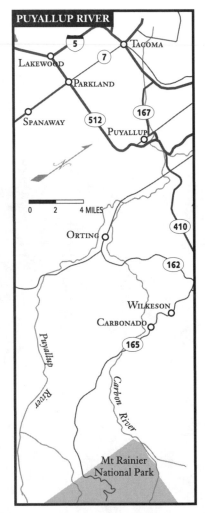

The route of Tolmie's botanizing trip in 1833, first European to set foot on slopes of Rainier (Tahoma?).

The White River issuing from Emmons and Winthrop Glaciers, the Carbon River from Carbon Glacier, the Mowich River from Mowich Glacier, and the Puyallup from Tahoma and Puyallup Glaciers, all flow as one to Commencement Bay, the sum of the rock-milky melt, snowfield trickles, and rain-fed springs from the entire northeast and north and most of the west slopes of The Mountain. One wants to be respectfully humble when discussing this mighty river. Down it from the White 5800 years ago rumbled or squished the Osceola Mudflow. And down the Puyallup proper a mere 600 years ago the Electron Mudflow buried Orting under 15 feet of boulders and muck; floods devastated the rest of the valley, dumping 5 feet of mud at Sumner. Another bad day for the Indians.

Loop trip: 1½ miles
High point: 200 feet
Elevation gain: none
Map: 41

Northernmost of the eight fingers of Commencement Bay reaching into the Puyallup River delta, the Hylebos Waterway is the dredged-out lower extremity of Hylebos Creek. Fortuitous accidents preserved the wetlands at headwaters of the West Fork. Then came Francis and Ilene Marcks to make life so uncomfortable for public officials that in 1981, starting with a gift of land from the Marcks, they conceded a state park.

A loop trail and side paths exhibit the wonders. Huge old Sitka spruce—one of the smaller trees was cored and found to date from 1662. A sand boil, the dance of grains mesmerizing the susceptible into a trance.

Look for quaking bogs with Labrador tea and kalmia and swamp birch; big western red cedar and hemlock (only one corner of the park was logged, in the nineteenth century) and a fallen Pacific yew (an estimated 500-1000 years old), Oregon ash, and cottonwood; the deep sinks, a pole provided to let you measure the depth (17 feet!) for yourself, and giving an air to the scene by bubbling up fumes of sulphur gas. The tally of birds is 114 species, of mammals in the dozens, flowers (uncounted), shrubs (18), mosses (25), liverworts (6), lichens (18), plus fungi,

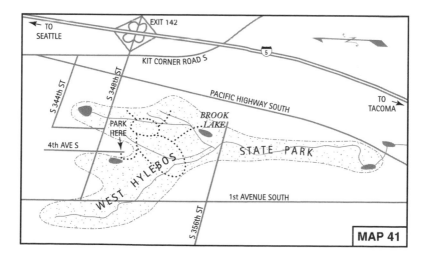

and "unidentified aquatic forms" (the Loch Ness Monster?).

Returned from the loop, visit the display, "Beginning Growth of Fossil-Related Trees," including the Gingko and dawn redwood formerly native to Washington; Man Lake, to see Canada geese, ringnecks, golden eyes, buffleheads, wood ducks, and nearly every local waterfowl; and the arboretum, containing three of every conifer found in the state (23 in all) and a variety of rhododendrons.

Directions: *Drive I-5 to Exit 142B, signed "Federal Way," and go off on 348 Street. Pass three stoplights, the last at 9 Avenue S. In a long block from there turn left on 4 Avenue S, signed "West Hylebos Wetlands State Park," past a couple houses to a "Parking" sign. Elevation, 220 feet.*

SWAN CREEK CANYON PARK

Round trip: 5 miles
High point: 200 feet
Elevation gain: 180 feet
Map: 42

Directions: *Drive I-5 to Exit 135 and go off to Highway 167, following "Puyallup" signs. Well out of the interchange, diverge right on Pioneer Way. In 0.7 mile, just before Waller Road, note a chain-closed lane signed "Swan Creek Trail," entry to a Tacoma–Pierce County park of 200-plus acres. Park on the wide shoulder near the gate, elevation 20 feet.*

A wildland's value varies inversely with the square of the distance from home. What would be merely nice in the heart of a national park is beyond price in your backyard. Thus is magnified the preciousness of Swan Creek Canyon, a refuge of green wild peace on the exact city limits of Tacoma.

Follow the lane through pastures and orchard into woods. As the

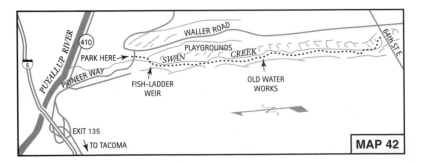

canyon is entered the roars and growls and belches and sneezes of civilization are muted, letting through to the walker's ear the creek chatter and bird babble. In a scant ¼ mile the way touches the creek, here flowing over a fish-ladder weir. Though the road-trail continues, cross the weir to trail nicely graded but defensively constructed to exclude wheels.

Now beside the gravel-rattling creek, now contouring high on the sidehill, the upsy-downsy path ascends the valley in the snug isolation of a spacious wild living room, a green grotto under arching maples and alders. The way burrows through vine maple, passes

Swan Creek Canyon

> *As the canyon is entered the roars and growls and belches and sneezes of civilization are muted, letting through to the walker's ear the creek chatter and bird babble.*

giant cedar stumps, trickling tributaries. The forest floor and understory are an arboretum—skunk cabbage and maidenhair fern, youth-on-age and ginger, devil's club and elderberry. Of historical interest are relics of an ancient waterworks—wire-wrapped wooden pipes, mossy concrete cisterns, and a springhouse. (Additional historic interest: Under an older name, "Bummer Gulch," the canyon was Tacoma's largest hobo jungle.)

The creek dwindles, the canyon narrows. At a long 2 miles the trail ends, where an old road (for pioneers' wagons?) once dipped into the canyon to cross. Hippety-hop over the creek and proceed on lesser trail a final scant ½ mile to trail's practical end where the creek flows in a culvert under 64 Street. In all this distance not a house is to be seen and the rantings and ravings of civilization are far away.

SNAKE LAKE NATURE CENTER

Three loop trips 3 miles
High point: 423 feet
Elevation gain: 150 feet
Map: 43

Directions: *Go off I-5 on Exit 132 to Highway 16. In 2.7 miles turn right on South 19th Street. At South Tyler Street turn right and then immediately left into Snake Lake Nature Center, elevation 300 feet.*

Snake Lake is interesting on several counts. For one, it is not notable for snakes—the name is for the shape. Second, it is fed by a 1200-acre watershed to the north—the streets of Tacoma! Water that once filtered through swamps and marshes over weeks and months now flushes through the pipes in hours. As a consequence, the lake is changing in character from open to closed—to marshes and swamps. The city uses it as a detention basin to regulate flow down Flett Creek to Chambers Creek. Third (and hurrah!), the 54-acre reserve of the Metropolitan Park District of Tacoma has been set aside as an ecological study area. "The park is not a playground. The visitor is reminded that the park belongs to the plants and animals. People are visitors in their space." Some twenty species of mammals can be found here, from red fox to flying squirrel to voles and shrews. Birds—more than one hundred species. Ten pairs of wood ducks nest at the lake.

> *Some twenty species of mammals can be found here, from red fox to flying squirrel to voles and shrews.*

The short loop is from the parking lot to the Heron (first) Bridge, loop trip ½ mile.

The medium loop goes down the west side of the lake to Blackbird (second) Bridge, crosses, and returns on the east side of the lake-swamp along the old grade of the Tacoma–Lake City Railway, built in 1890 from Old Tacoma to a resort on American Lake, way way out in the country. The route returns to Heron Bridge, where the wood ducks were hanging out, and to the parking lot. Loop trip, 1 mile.

The longest loop is the bestest. It sets out down the west side of the swamp-lake, passing shelters for birders, and goes under the freeway bridge to Mallard (third) Bridge and Cottonwood Shelter. Next, back to Blackbird Bridge, across and up switchbacks from wetlands habitat to forest habitats, through Douglas fir, madrona, and a few Pacific dogwood. The trail tops out at 423 feet, soon after passing a kettle left behind by the glacier some 12,000 years ago. The descent passes a few Oregon white oak on the way back to Heron Bridge and the parking. Loop trip, 1¾ miles.

The self-guiding pamphlet explains the bee tree, black cottonwood, cascara buckthorn, bitter cherry, poison hemlock, Goose Prairie (mowed for the Canada geese), filberts, green heron, open water

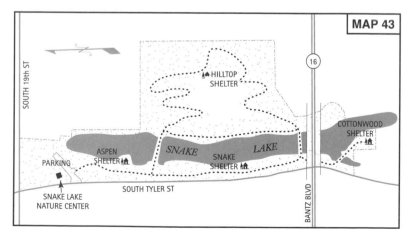

in scoops dug out by peat-mining, an ancient ant hill, and the greater yellowlegs. Fun and instruction for the whole family. (But be *quiet*, children.)

TACOMA-TO-TAHOMA TRAIL (THAT COULD BE)

A walker of today must have catholic tastes in scenery and some ingenuity in routefinding to retrace Tolmie's trip. I did bits and pieces and feel the better for it, more resonant with how the water would feel about itself, if it felt. There's much good along the way. Views across

Ezra Meekers Mansion in Puyallup

murky waters to the far glaciers—this is one of only three outlets of The Mountain's water, the others being the Nisqually and Cowlitz Rivers. History. The site of Fort Maloney, built in February 1856 by the U.S. Army to protect the John Carson ferry, thought necessary after Indian attacks of the previous October. Here the Military Road from Steilacoom to Bellingham crossed the river. For more history, in Puyallup visit Pioneer Park and the restored 17-room mansion of Ezra Meeker, who arrived in Puget Sound by wagon train in 1852 and platted the town in 1877. The junction with the White–Stuck River at the route's entry into the Big Valley of Pleistocene time. The transition backward in time to the past-lingering-in-present—a farming valley, fields of crops and cows, old homes and barns, little old country stores. Of course, the 7-11s are coming. Tacoma is coming.

PORT OF TACOMA

Round trip: 11 miles
High point: 20 feet
Elevation gain: none
Maps: 44A, 44B

The best grimy-industrial trip in the book, this walk over the Puyallup delta is most exciting on a workday when all the satanic contraptions are bumping and grinding and honking and bellowing, infernally fascinating. Yet serenely sliding through is the river, green-brown from pollution by glaciers and farms, afloat with ducks and gulls and fishermen, but not with ships because the river—or Puyallup Waterway as the final stretch is called—is rarely used for docking; a half-dozen busier waterways are dredged in delta silt.

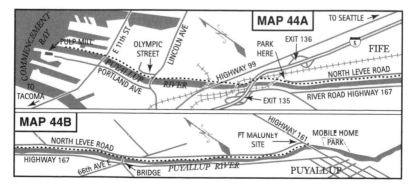

Directions: *Drive Highway 167 to about halfway between I-5 and Puyallup. Between mileposts 3 and 4, at 66 Avenue E, turn north over the river on narrow old Melroy Bridge. Turn east on North Levee Road and drive 3 miles to its end at a railroad bridge. Park here, elevation 20 feet.*

Cross the railroad tracks, drop to the dike, and away you go downstream. The levee is unobstructed, the gravel road little used. This is the premier walk for bridges, some old, some new, some supported by piers of wood or concrete, others on concrete pillars. In sequence there are a railroad bridge, I-5 monster bridge, another railroad bridge, old Highway 99 bridge, a third rail bridge (there's a lot of good train-watching), Lincoln Avenue Bridge, a fourth rail bridge (this a swing-opener to let ships through), and finally the classic 11 Street Bridge, with a tower-lift center section.

Along the way are views to downtown Tacoma on the bluffs above the delta. At the end are views over the bay to ships coming and going and sitting at anchor, and to Point Defiance, Vashon and Maury Islands, and the Olympics. Also at the end is the star entertainment— the Katzenjammer Kastle pulp mill, hissing, squealing, humming, and roaring, pouring clouds of steam from a dozen stacks and a hundred cracks in the walls.

BIG VALLEY'S END

Round trip: downstream from the Canyon to Carbon River
    confluence 16 miles
High point: 350 feet
Elevation gain: none
Map: 45

Take a moment to think upstream. Don't walk. I did all 3½ miles to Electron, but that was before the quiet log railroad to Lake Kapowsin was replaced by a thundering truck road. The Electron Mudflow was not caused by, but was named for, Puget Power's Electron Power-

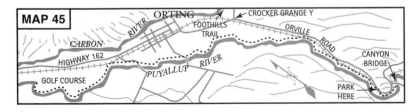

house. A cog railway once carried tourists up the Kapowsin Scarp to a vista point beside the reservoir. This was a pretty impressive hydroelectric operation for 1904.

From cottonwood forest the river emerges to farms and sorties out to the middle of the broad plain.

The Electron Flume enters the reservoir, often carrying most of the Puyallup River from the Headworks weir 10 miles upstream. My expedition up the plank walkway on the steep and jungled wild side of the valley was aborted by umbrella weather that made the planks treacherous. From the Headworks, logging roads approximate the Tolmie route to where he (presumably) left the valley floor to climb into meadows of today's Mount Rainier National Park.

Now, to the walk.

Directions: *Drive Highway 162 southeast of Orting 1 mile, and at the Crocker Grange Y, turn south on Orville Road. In 3.3 miles, as road and river are partway through a horseshoe bend where Orville Road bridges the river, park on a large shoulder, elevation 350 feet.*

Drop to the gravel lane below the road. Follow it down to a lane entering from the highway. Turn downstream on the abandoned rail grade. You're on your way. The dike goes on and on, crossed by frequent stock fences easily circumvented. Except for the occasional farm vehicle, wheels rarely roll the road.

At the start the Puyallup valley is canyon—narrow, soon widening to a modest floodplain, then abruptly to a mile from green wall to green wall, the veritable Big Valley. Cows moo, dogs bark, guns of Fort Lewis boom. From cottonwood forest the river emerges to farms and sorties out to the middle of the broad plain. Off east can be seen the Carbon valley, Microwave Hill and Spar Pole Hill, and—gasp—Tahoma.

Gravel bars and beaches of black volcanic sand are alternatives to the dike. Marshes and sloughs are passed, barns and more cows, and, at a scant 4 miles, the bridge of the Orting-Kapowsin Road, which due to fences is not an access.

Now, the best part. The river turns westward to the foot of the high, steep wild-forested valley wall and at a scant 2 miles from the bridge reaches Hi Cedars Golf Club. For 1 long mile the neat greensward is on one side of the dike, the river and green-tangled wall on the other. Where Orting High students of the Class of 1941 put their numbers on a boulder (as have other classes on other boulders the entire route) is the proper turnaround. It is 1 more mile to the Carbon confluence, made unpleasant by hellberries. The main attraction is the boulder of the Class of 1937.

FOOTHILLS "TRAIL"

Maps: 46A–46C

Cued by the nationwide Rails-to-Trails movement, the Pierce County Parks Department began implementing a citizen-driven plan to put feet, hooves, and bicycles on the abandoned 21 miles of the Burlington-Northern Railroad from McMillin to Orting to Crocker to South Prairie to Buckley.

The multi-use travelway is always close to public roads shown on highway maps and thus the only information a person needs is that it exists. (Or will when human obstacles are removed.) It surely will be renowned as a bikeway from the Big Valley to footings of The Mountain.

A pedestrian values it most as access to a series of wheelfree gravel

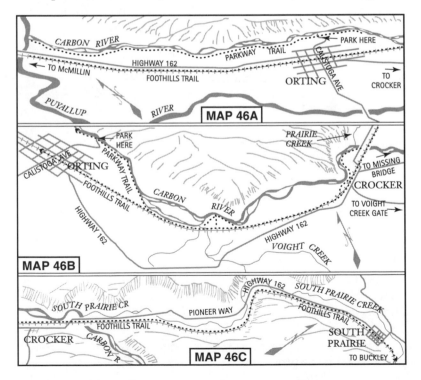

bars, sandbars tracked by deer and ducks and raccoons. My favorite isn't on the route at all, but begins in Orting and follows dikes and bars of the Carbon River downstream 2¾ miles to its confluence with the Puyallup. A gravel peninsula thrusts out to a tip between the Puyallup, often yellow-green with rock milk while the Carbon is crystal clear—or sometimes chocolate-brown with rock flour.

CARBON RIVER PARKWAY TRAIL (THAT COULD BE)
Maps: 47A, 47B, 48A–48C

In 1869, inventorying the booty heisted five years earlier in the Northern Pacific Land Grant, railroad surveyors found sandstone and coal on a tributary of the Carbon River. From the company treasurer the resulting town took its name, Wilkeson. The place reeks of history, a century and more of artifacts lurking in the bushes. And it's pretty, too. To better enjoy the town and its surroundings, read Carbon River Coal Country, by Nancy Irene Hall.

Muse through the cemetery; there's another off the highway on Johns Road. Poke into side streets for nineteenth-century architecture, including the handsome building signed "Holy Trinity Orthodox Church in America 1900." At the far edge of town turn left onto Railroad Avenue, past the striking Wilkeson sandstone school.

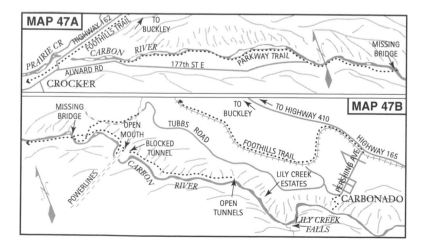

Old railroad tunnel on Carbon River Parkway Trail

The main attraction of the town nowadays is the region's largest quarry, off-limits to visitors unless prior arrangements are made. However, there is no objection to walkers politely following the road of Wilkeson Cut Stone Company ¼ mile from Railroad Avenue to the fringe of the stone-cutting works. The quarry can be glimpsed, far up the hill. Overhead cables (used to) bring monster slabs down to the shed where gangsaws patiently cut into the stone at the rate of 4 inches an hour. The first use of the stone was by the railroad, for fill and riprap, widely utilized around the region. In 1883–84 the first stone was taken out for construction—of St. Luke's Episcopal Church in Tacoma. A man named Walker quarried blocks from 1911 on, taking them to Tacoma by rail for splitting. In 1915 the present plant was built, the machinery pretty much devised on the spot by self-taught engineers, a time-warp trip to early days of the Industrial Revolution. Until the 1920s, most Seattle streets were paved with Wilkeson cobblestones. In 1982 the company went bankrupt and the quarry was closed, whether permanently or not remains to be seen.

In 1881 Bailey Willis opened a tourists' horse trail to the Carbon River from Wilkeson, and the next year cut a way over the ridge to the Mowich and the Puyallup, where he erected the cluster of log cabins grandly called Palace Camp. Prospectors later built a spur to Mowich Lake and Spray Park; a grindstone they left at the spur junction gave it the name of Grindstone Trail. When the railroad was extended to new mines farther up the Carbon, the Bailey Willis Trail became known as the Fairfax Trail, ultimately extended through Puyallup country to the Nisqually River.

Except for bits in the national park, the old trail system—here and throughout the Carbon province—has been obliterated by logging. Hikers long ago gave it up as a lost cause and herded into the park.

The 1979 predecessor of this book, *Footsore 4*, propounded a great notion:

"Here is a green-jungle, white-water lane of lonesome wildness reaching out from Mount Rainier National Park nearly to the lowlands. The gorgeous gorge and splendid forest, the colorful rocks, both sedimentary and volcanic, the foaming cataracts, the old coal mines and coke ovens and vanished villages are at an elevation open to walking the year around. What to do with them? How about a Parkway Trail? Connected to the Tacoma-to-Tahoma Trail? A continuous route from saltwater to volcano icefields. The Whulge to The Mountain!

"Look from Seattle/Tacoma to Mount Rainier. The footings of The Mountain itself are hidden by Carbon Ridge, whose peaks are, west to east, Burnt Mountain, Old Baldy, "Old Nameless," and— highest and most prominent—the half-horn of 5933-foot Pitcher Mountain, which everybody sees and nobody has ever heard of."

OTHER TRIPS
Map: 49

Pitcher Mountain. The footings of Rainier are concealed from Seattle by Carbon Ridge, whose highest and most distinctive summit is the half-horn of 5933-foot Pitcher Mountain. Views extend from glaciers of The Mountain to waters of Whulge. Walk logging roads above South Prairie Creek to the edge of the Clearwater Wilderness.

South Prairie Ridge. Logging roads out of Wilkeson climb to a boggling desolation of clear-cuts far up onto the mass of Mount Rainier.

Sparpole Hill. Marked by the spar pole of the 1910 railroad logging, its views reopened by the second-growth clearcutting of 1977, this final blip of Ptarmigan Ridge long was the classic mountain-edge walk of the Kapowsin Tree Farm. When that boodle of the Big Steal was sold to Champion, the popularity of Sparpole dropped to zero. That is, via the $10 gate. The old entry via Voight Creek Gate is being remembered and the popularity restored, as is that of adjoining Microwave Hill. Powerlines are a handy way to dodge around the gate onto Fox Creek Road, which leads to Beane Creek Road, and thence through old stumps and new to the spar pole and the 360-degree panorama.

A person can experience a religious transport gazing over the broad, flat valley where Mowich and Puyallup Rivers and Niesson Creek join to 13,000 feet of icefalls and lava ramparts.

Confluence of the Mowich and Puyallup Rivers. An upside-down hike, starting in a descent from old Camp 2 (still older, Grindstone Camp) to the Momentous Union. The view of 12,000 vertical feet of The Mountain is considered, by the few hikers who have seen it, to be the most stupendous Rainier picture there is.

Evans Peak. The 5000-foot westernmost summit of the "Park Boundary Peaks." Nothing in the way to block views to the Big Valley and Seattle.

St. Paul Lookout. By driving the Camp 1 Road to or near Camp 1 (Ohop), then dodging around the fence onto the Main Road and

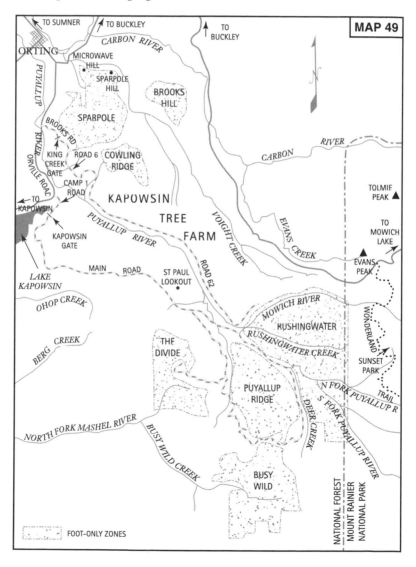

MAP 49

finding the little old abandoned side road to the lookout site at 2970 feet, a person can experience a religious transport gazing over the broad, flat valley where Mowich and Puyallup Rivers and Niesson Creek join (and where the Electron Mudflow did flow) to 13,000 feet of icefalls and lava ramparts (and a foreground of seventeen googols of stumps).

NISQUALLY RIVER

NISQUALLY RIVER

Management: State Parks, Tacoma Parks, University of Washington
Topographic maps: USGS Nisqually, Weir Prairie, Harts Lake, Bald Hill, Tanwax Creek, Eatonville, Ohop Valley, Mineral, Morton, Kapowsin, Mount Wow—and their equivalents in the Green Trails series, privately published

Southernmost of Rainier's great ice-melts to enter Whulge, for generations the world's way to The Mountain. The state, since 1987, has been creating a parkway from the National Park to the National Wildlife Refuge of the delta.

When I walked the *Footsore* series in the 1970s, my notion was to survey day hikes whose trailheads lay within a two-hour round-trip drive of Puget Sound City. Sad to say, the gridlock of the new millennium has put the South Puget Plain, Ohop Creek, Mashel River, and the Nisqually Parkway-in-creation beyond the pale.

However, day hikes have no parallel elsewhere in the Puget Trough. Leave home early, before the commute hour, and expect to return home late, after the commute hour.

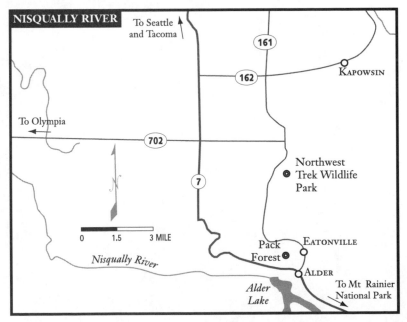

Round trip: 10 miles
High point: 760 feet
Elevation gain: none
Map: 50

No zoo, this, but a unique 645-acre wildlife park of Tacoma Metropolitan Park District, maintained in cooperation with Tacoma Zoological Society. Northwest Trek was begun by the loving care of Dr. David and Constance Hellyer, who acquired the property in 1937 and in 1972 gave it to the public. Hundreds of thousands of visitors a year take the 5½-mile, 1-hour Trek Tour, riding quiet trams through areas where animals roam free—only people are fenced in. The park is open daily February through October, Wednesdays and weekends November to January.

Directions: *Drive Highway 161 south from Puyallup toward Eatonville. (Or, drive Highway 7 south from Tacoma and at a Trek sign opposite Highway 702 jog to 161.) Just south of Clear Lake turn in on the park entrance and drive 0.7 mile to parking areas from which paths lead to Trek Center, elevation 760 feet.*

Take the Trek Tour to see deer, elk, moose, woodland caribou, bison, wolverine, bighorn sheep, mountain goat, and Pennsylvania wild turkey roaming gone-to-nature farm fields and second-growth wildland woods.

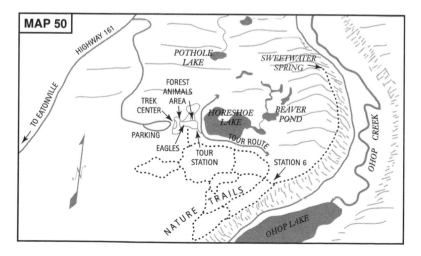

Do some walking, too, on the 5 miles of nature trails; these are in a different area from that of the tour, which cannot be visited on foot. For openers, near the main entrance is Cat Country, pairs of bobcat, cougar, and lynx. Left from the center is a loop of blacktop paths totaling ½ mile, passing animals in natural habitats (beaver, porcupine, otter, fisher, mink, skunk, weasel, marten, raccoon, a children's Baby Animal Exhibit, and—supreme thrill—an overlook of nonchalant bear—and wolves loping through woodland).

For the long walk, go right from the center toward the Tour Station above Horseshoe Lake, beyond which loom summit snows of Rainier. On the way, opposite uncaged, unchained bald eagles and golden eagles perching there watching the parade, is the trailhead. From it are a number of loops of various lengths, sampling the various forest systems—marsh, young fir, alder-maple. For an introductory tour, do the perimeter loop, taking all right turns, and thus in about 1 mile reach the brink of the plateau, the Ohop valley scarp, and screened glimpses of Ohop Lake. In about ⅓ mile more, at Station 6, starts a side trip, the best part. Turn right and proceed along the bluff in cool green lush forest, past the end of Ohop Lake, out along the slope of Goat Ridge, to Sweetwater Spring, 1 mile from the loop. Sit a while, imagine how sweet it was (before the Great Giardiasis Pandemic) to dip a delicious sip or so from the boxed-in pool. Return to Station 6. Again on the perimeter, return to the eagles in a final ⅔ mile.

Elk at Northwest Trek

Dress and behave appropriately and you may be taken for one of the exhibits, as was I, eagerly asked by a party of foreigners, "Sir, are you a logger?" The honor modestly accepted, there is now some corner of England where my photo is displayed as representative of the species.

PACK FOREST

Map: 51

At the interface of lowlands and foothills, on a "mountain island" enclosed by Mashel and Nisqually Rivers, is Pack Forest, a 4400-acre laboratory of the University of Washington's College of Forest Resources. Miles and miles of lonesome foot-roads wind around hills and valleys in woodland and meadow and views from Rainier to Puget Sound. Snowline-probing and animal tracks in winter, flowers in spring and summer, colors and mushrooms in fall. And—peace be with you— on weekends the gates are closed to public wheels, but not feet.

Aside from pedestrian pleasures, Pack is a unique opportunity to observe a wide range of forest-management techniques and experiments. Tree-farming was pioneered here, including some of the earliest plantations in the Northwest. Thinning began in 1930, and in the 1940s the first forest-fertilization studies anywhere in the world. Through the years there have been programs in forest nutrition and in harvesting methods, clear-cut and shelterwood. The largest research project ever undertaken at Pack Forest is a twenty-year study of the effects of recycling biosolids as a forest fertilizer. ("Biosolids" are treated wastewater solids, as distinguished from untreated "sludge.") It was for such purposes that Charles Lathrop Pack made the initial gift of land in 1926, establishing a teaching and research laboratory for teachers and students, a demonstration area for the forest industry, and, for the general public, a living textbook.

The andesite ridges of Pack, glacial drift-covered down low, rock-outcropping up high, were thoroughly burned about 1800, only a few relict trees escaping. Some of this 1800 forest survived

Miles and miles of lonesome foot-roads wind around hills and valleys in woodland and meadow and views from Rainier to Puget Sound.

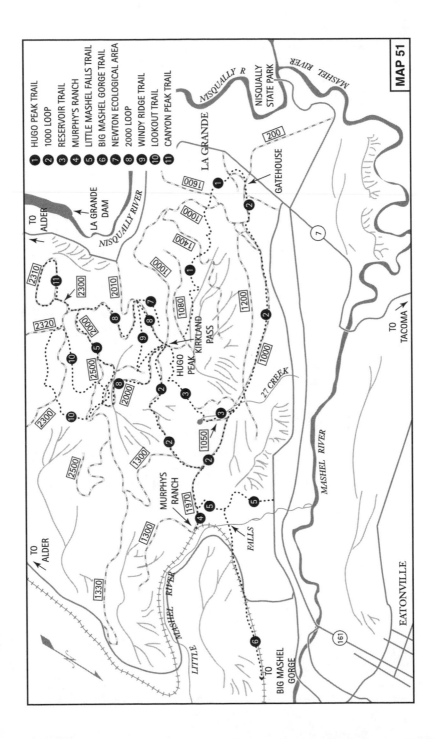

MAP 51

1 HUGO PEAK TRAIL
2 1000 LOOP
3 RESERVOIR TRAIL
4 MURPHY'S RANCH
5 LITTLE MASHEL FALLS TRAIL
6 BIG MASHEL GORGE TRAIL
7 NEWTON ECOLOGICAL AREA
8 2000 LOOP
9 WINDY RIDGE TRAIL
10 LOOKOUT TRAIL
11 CANYON PEAK TRAIL

Pack Forest nature trail

the big Eatonville Fire of 1926 and other blazes of the period. A management plan has been adopted to increase age diversification of Pack's forest groups and thus enhance the educational value: 10 percent of the land, including the 42-acre relict-tree Ecological Area, will be reserved in a natural state; 14 percent, including the 940-acre Hugo Peak Transect of 1800 forest, will be specially managed, only limited salvage logging of fire-damaged trees; and 76 percent, including the almost two-thirds of Pack burned since 1920, will be intensively managed on a conifer rotation of eighty years, approximately 30 acres to be harvested annually. A single walk passes trees from seedling age to centuries old and a variety of planting and tending and harvesting methods.

Change is a constant at Pack Forest. Roads are improved or built; each year clear-cuts open new views—as the growth in plantations is closing old ones. Pack, however, is much more than a cellulose factory. Though 95 percent self-supporting from harvesting, the income is incidental to the teaching, the research, and the "demonstration," which is so integral to the purposes that visitors are not merely tolerated but warmly welcomed. The hiker is as much a part of the picture as the forester.

When the gate is open to public vehicles, a straight-out car tour appeals to young and old, pausing for close looks, taking short walks. On weekends, the gate closed, Pack Forest becomes a de facto wilderness (except that bicycles are permitted on roads—but *not* on trail-trails) and hikes must be done from the gate.

Pick up a (free) map at the gatehouse, showing all the roads and trails—and giving their current numbers, which change from time to time, and may not be the same as in this book. Especially if kids are in the party, tour the 1:100-scale miniature Pack Forest at the entrance.

HUGO PEAK

Round trip: from gate 5 miles
High point: 1740 feet
Elevation gain: 950 feet
Map: 51

Directions: *Drive Highway 161 through Eatonville to Highway 7 (or drive 7 direct from Tacoma). At 0.2 mile south on 7 from the junction is the Pack Forest entry. At the gate (open weekdays to 4:30 p.m., closed weekends) is the parking area, elevation 800 feet.*

Find the Hugo Peak trailhead on the right opposite the gatehouse, elevation 800 feet, and begin a gentle ascent through a plantation. In ½ mile pass the Hugo Peak Connector Trail, going ½ mile left to the headquarters buildings through a stand of thinned Douglas fir. The Hugo Peak Trail proceeds in a variety of forest stands, crossing road No. 1000, 1040 feet.

In the 2 miles from road No. 1000 (on weekdays, an alternate trailhead, for a 4-mile round trip), the way steepens into a beauty of a mixed forest, switchbacks on old roads-trails, to road No. 1801. A sign, "Hugo Peak," points left to road No. 1080, where another sign leads to the highest point, 1740 feet.

Beyond are the Nisqually, Bald Hills, and woods and farms and lakes of the South Puget Plain.

Located at the exact abrupt front of the Cascades, since being partially clearcut in 1974 to salvage trees dying from fire damage, the summit plateau of Hugo has been the classic grandstand of Pack Forest. From the 1740-foot peak, and the 1720-foot peak, and the 1693-foot peak, are views. Below is the Mashel valley, the Ohop valley joining from the north. Beyond are the Nisqually, Bald Hills, and woods and farms and lakes of the South Puget Plain, over which Nisqually and Deschutes Rivers run to Nisqually Reach and Budd Inlet, respectively. Beyond saltwaterways rise Black Hills and Olympics. The pulp mill steam plume marks Tacoma. The Issaquah Alps point to Seattle.

1000 LOOP

Loop trip: 5¼ miles plus 2 miles round trip from gate (all side trips total 10 miles more)
High point: 1593 feet
Elevation gain: (loop only) 900 feet
Map: 51

The main road of Pack Forest, a grand loop around Hugo Peak, is Lathrop Drive, road No. 1000, a splendid "trail" (when the gate is closed) walk by itself, and a very full day for the long-leggity if all the sidetrips noted here are taken. These will not be described in detail here. See our map. Also, don't be surprised by other side trips, newly created or left undescribed to save for you the joy of discovery.

Directions: *Drive Highway 161 through Eatonville to Highway 7 (or drive 7 direct from Tacoma). At 0.2 mile south on 7 from the junction is the Pack Forest entry. At the gate (open weekdays to 4:30 p.m., closed weekends) is the parking area, elevation 800 feet.*

To do the loop clockwise, walk left from the administration building, signed "Lathrop Drive, Murphy's Ranch." Pass above the millpond of the former sawmill and proceed along the road through forest experimentally treated with municipal sewage sludge in 1977, pioneer project in the system now being employed on forest lands throughout the region, and then a plantation of 1978. Cross 27 Creek and at 1½ miles from the administration building come to a sign on the right, "1050 Road."

Reservoir Trail, round trip 1½ miles. Turn right on road No. 1050 to the 27 Creek Reservoir, intended by the CCC to provide water for fighting fires, now an abandoned, moody, black pool. The trail ascends ¾ mile to Kirkland Pass.

Back on 1000: A scant ½ mile from 27 Creek is a Y at the forest edge, 1160 feet, and the takeoff of three side trips, any of which would by itself finish off the day, hang the loop.

Murphy's Ranch, round trip 1½ miles. Rainier's huge whiteness ambushes the eye. Go left on road No. 1970 into the broad pastures of 650-acre Murphy's Ranch, which under the name of Flying M Ranch was famed in the 1960s for rock concerts and in 1975 was acquired by Pack Forest.

Little Mashel Falls, round trip 1½ miles. Walk ⅓ mile on road No. 1970 to the far end of an experimental plantation of cottonwoods. At the end of a fence look left for a muddy track through the grass, start of the Falls Trail, which winds down the hill. At the foot of the hill, ignore a path continuing straight ahead and turn right into mixed forest. A flat stretch comes to a Y, an old road-trail straight right, the trail to the left. The roar of the falls grows loud and the way soon arrives at the top of Bridal Veil Falls (the middle and largest) and enchanting deep pools below the upper, or Tom Tom Falls. From Tom Tom, a path can be found upstream to a lovely little falls.

Return up the trail and watch on the right for an obscure track that drops down, down, down—slippery, slippery. Bridal Veil comes in view—wowee! Slip-slide on and down to a promontory ridge between the middle and lower falls. Turn right to the rock-slab pools at the base of Bridal Veil Falls. Walk behind the falls in a rock shelter. Roar, water, roar!

No safe route can be seen down to the lowest falls. Be satisfied.

Or not. The former road entry, from the highway to Murphy's Ranch, dwindled to a trail, crosses the river to the new (since 1944) grade of the Tacoma Eastern Railroad, which once upon a time was the primary tourist route from Tacoma to Elbe and The Mountain. On the far side find a path down the mossy, flowers-in-spring rock slot the river has sliced to the uppermost falls. Carefully pick a slick way by potholes to the plunge basin.

Little Mashel Falls

Now for the real action. Return on the tracks 150 feet from the bridge and spot a dirt track up the cutbank. Follow the trail along the gorge rim. Rude paths go off left to poor looks down to the middle falls, but they're nothing much. The main tread leads to the top of the lower falls. There's something, okay. Arched over by maples, the stream flows on lichen-dark, water-rounded, exquisitely sculptured rock, down a small cataract into a black pool of foam-flecked mountain tea. There it gathers itself and hurls over the brink—to a preliminary drop, then out of sight in the forbidding chasm. Gracious. At one time or another Eatonville got water from here and toyed with a ridiculous hydroelectric scheme, but now the falls area is preserved in Pack Forest.

The bottom of the lower falls—actually a double falls totaling about 150 feet—can be reached by a perilous skidway. Not yet satisfied? In a ½-mile gorge the Little Mashel drops 270 more feet. That ought to do it.

Arched over by maples, the stream flows on lichen-dark, water-rounded, exquisitely sculptured rock, down a small cataract into a black pool of foam-flecked mountain tea.

Big Mashel Gorge, round trip 4 miles. The forest walk 1 mile upstream on the grade of the Tacoma Eastern is pretty. Downstream is the spectacularity. In a long 1 mile from the Little Mashel, the grade rounds a nose of lichen-black rock, a garden of alumroot, ocean spray, and goatsbeard. Ever seen a town nestle? That's what Eatonville does, in the Mashel valley, amid its hills. Look across to the fabulous Ohop Wall, turn around to see Hugo Peak, and gaze down to the site of the Eatonville sawmill that closed some sixty years ago. Over lowlands are Bald Hills and Black Hills.

In 1 more mile is the Big Mashel River. Just before the bridge, skid down the embankment to river level and follow a woods road to the gorge. Lordy. Downstream the river widens to pools of what is merely a nice wild river. Upstream, though, it tumbles from a slot gorge through which mountain tea flows in black deeps as narrow as 4 feet wide under cliffs 200 feet high.

Back on 1000: From the 1160-foot Y proceed upward. Forest grown since the 1926 and other fires abruptly yields to wonderful big trees of the 1800 forest, plus a few older relics. Note fire damage to the big trees, many of which are nearing death—thus the salvage logging. In 1¼ miles, gaining 460 feet, is the Pack hub, Kirkland Pass, 1593 feet. Five roads come to the pass, all plainly signed.

Newton Ecological Area, round trip 1 mile. This is mandatory—the 42-acre Ecological Area through 1800 forest, tall trees and deep shadows. In the heart of the area are relicts from a more ancient past. Walk the Trail of the Giants down the valley of usually waterless Newton Creek. The trail branches, forming a loop. Don't go fast, take your time—time to feel the dimensions of giant hemlocks and cedars and Douglas firs up to 9 feet in diameter, 250 feet tall, maybe 450 years old.

Hugo Peak, round trip ½ mile. From Kirkland pass, road No. 1080 gets you the summit, if you haven't already got it.

Back on 1000: Take the middle road, signed "Highway;" in ¾ mile leave the 1800 cathedral, pause at a 1981 salvage show for smashing views down to the drowned Nisqually Canyon and the La Grande Dam that done it, and at 2 miles from Kirkland Pass close the loop.

OTHER TRIPS

The Divide (map 52). Had the physical entirety (not to mention the Greater Ecosystem) of Rainier been put in the national park, America would come here to pay respects as it does at Paradise and Sunrise. A spur from Weyerhaeuser road No. 6000 ascends to 3370-foot Beetle Peak, named for the vehicle that attained the summit at the venerable age of 105,926 miles, many spent surveying the four *Footsores*, and now in deserved retirement on Cougar Mountain. An elk trail connects ⅓ downhill mile from one company's scalping roads to the other; in 4 miles from Beetle Peak the 4100-foot Top Top is reached.

Busy Wild Mountain (map 53). Forest Service road No. 59 climbs from Highway 706 to the edge of the Kapowsin Tree Farm at 4200 feet. In 1 mile on logging roads is Copper Knob, 4850 feet, nary a bush left to anchor the slimy volcanic soils sloughing off this way to the Nisqually River, that way to Busy Wild Creek, tributary to the Mashel. In ¾ mile more are two little lakes in cozy little subalpine cirques. In 1½ more miles of satanic beauty of yellow-white mush from which the last trees were stripped in the early 1980s, the summit of 4850-foot

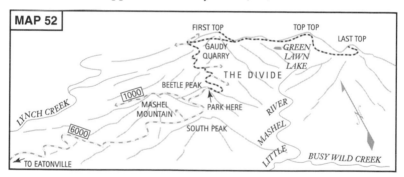

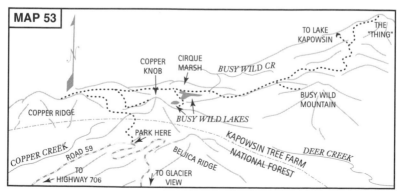

Busy Wild Mountain gives close views of The Mountain. Another 2½ miles lead to the summit of Thing Peak, 4930 feet, once the site of Puyallup Ridge Lookout, now the boggling-big Thing, apparently the Bell System relay to the rings of Saturn.

Stahl Mountain. An unfamiliar south-of-the-Nisqually view of Rainier from the site of an old fire lookout. Drive the Little Nisqually Road and spurs to the clear-cut frontier on the ridge crest. In 1978 a forest trail led 1 mile to the cliff-edge summit.

La Grande Canyon. The most spectacular section of the Nisqually between glacier and delta. But Tacoma City Light got there before us and drowned it. Then, perhaps after *Footsore 4* enormously increased the number of walkers come to see La Grande Dam (built in 1912, rebuilt in 1944) and finger-narrow La Grande Reservoir, the canyon it desecrated, and the 840,000 tons of concrete, 330 feet high, 1500 feet long, of Alder Dam, built in 1944, the electricians got busy and fenced off public accesses.

Mashel Massacre. One fine day in March of 1856 a doughty company of real estate speculators, calling themselves the Washington Mounted Rifles, mostly colonels, rode into a village on the Mashel, discovered the men were away, and vented their frustrated patriotism by murdering seventeen women and children. If the site can be identified, a trail would be appropriate, and an interpretive center.

THE SOUTHERN FRONTIER

THE SOUTHERN FRONTIER

Management: State Department of Natural Resources
Topographic maps: USGS Tumwater, Tenino—and their
equivalents in the Green Trails series, privately published

A foreign country, too far away to lightly trip around from homes in
Puget Sound City. And yet. . . .

Ends. Whulge ends, and its feeder streams; here is a momentous
hydrographic divide. From the Bald Hills flows the Deschutes, southernmost river of the Cascades to enter Puget Sound. Also from the
Bald Hills flows the Skookumchuck, which turns south to the Rainier-
born Cowlitz and thus the Columbia. But also from the Bald Hills
flows the Chehalis, joined from the prairies by the Black, the two
together nearly enwrapping the Black Hills and proceeding west to
Grays Harbor.

Ends. Here ended the Puget Lobe of the Cordilleran Ice Sheet.
A hiker from the north senses a peculiarity in the hills—they remind
of the Western Cascades of Oregon, the Ozarks, or the southern Ap-

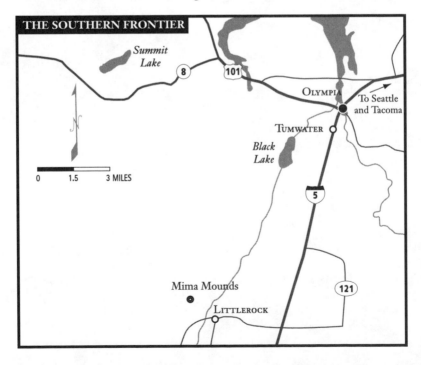

palachians. The reason is that the ice rode up the north flanks (on the east side of the Black Hills, to about 1460 feet) but not over the highest tops; the terrain is not ice-shaped and youthful—as say, the Issaquah Alps—but mainly stream-sculpted, maturely dissected.

The Puget–Willamette Trough continues south, but here where it narrows between Bald Hills–Black Hills "portals" are the enigmatic prairies. What is eastern Washington doing west of the crest? What are Oregon-like oak groves and western gray squirrels doing so far north? Tolmie in the 1840s remarked on the contrast with lush forests of uplands all around; declaring the prairies unsurpassed in elegance, he compared them to the open parks amid forests on artfully landscaped estates of English nobility. The art, of course, is Nature's. The flats are the outwash plains of rivers from the front of the ice in its farthest advance toward Oregon. The soil is composed of river gravels with poor water-retention; no matter that the skies are Puget Sound (drippy); so far as plants are concerned the sites are semi-arid.

Ends. Here the Really Big River carried ice-dammed waters of the Cascades through today's Chehalis valley to the ocean, joined west of the Black Hills by the Pretty Big River from the Olympics.

Ends. On prairies and their upland counterparts, the "balds," and in adjoining woodlands, are the northern limits of some plant species. And the southern limits of others.

Two trips must stand as representatives.

MIMA MOUNDS NATURAL AREA

Round trip: 1–5 miles
High point: 240 feet
Elevation gain: none
Map: 54

Directions: *Go off I-5 on Exit 95 and drive Highway 121 west to Littlerock. Proceed straight through on the road signed "Capitol Forest." Go right on Waddell Creek Road 0.7 mile and turn left to the parking area and trailhead, elevation 240 feet.*

A traveler in 1841 wondered at the pimples and at last declared, "In utter desperation I cease to trouble myself about their origin and call them the 'inexplicable mounds.'" Geologists took a try at explaining them as the result of freezing and thawing. Biologists compared them to "prairie mounds" of the Great Plains, and the "hogwallow

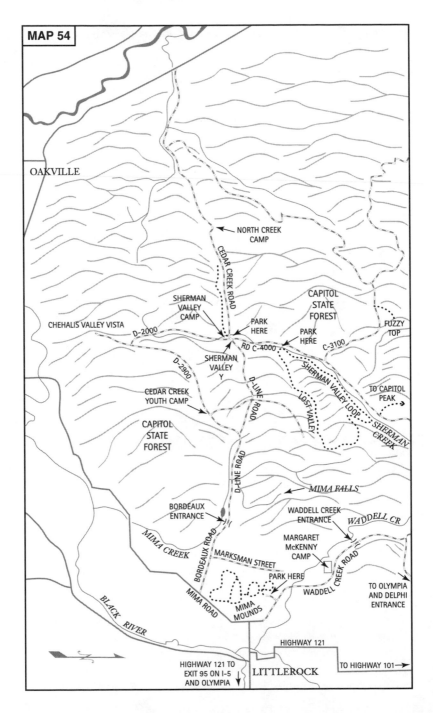

MAP 54

OAKVILLE

NORTH CREEK CAMP

CEDAR CREEK ROAD

SHERMAN VALLEY CAMP

PARK HERE

CAPITOL STATE FOREST

CHEHALIS VALLEY VISTA

D-2000

PARK HERE

RD C-4000

C-3100

FUZZY TOP

SHERMAN VALLEY Y

D-2900

D-LINE ROAD

SHERMAN VALLEY LOOP

TO CAPITOL PEAK

CEDAR CREEK YOUTH CAMP

LOST VALLEY

SHERMAN CREEK

CAPITOL STATE FOREST

D-LINE ROAD

MIMA FALLS

BORDEAUX ENTRANCE

WADDELL CREEK ENTRANCE

WADDELL CR

MARGARET McKENNY CAMP

MIMA CREEK

BORDEAUX ROAD

MARKSMAN STREET

WADDELL CREEK ROAD

TO OLYMPIA AND DELPHI ENTRANCE

PARK HERE

MIMA ROAD

MIMA MOUNDS

BLACK RIVER

HIGHWAY 121

HIGHWAY 121 TO EXIT 95 ON I-5 AND OLYMPIA

LITTLEROCK

TO HIGHWAY 101

country" of California. In 1991 Victor Scheffer and associates conclusively (insofar as anything in science ever is) established them as the work of pocket gophers now gone from this scene but still at their labors elsewhere west of the Mississippi and north of Mexico.

The spring flower show is famous—the grassland turns blue with camas blooms. In summer come the bluebells, wooly sunflowers, oxeye daisies.

Whatever, of the nearly 1,000,000 mounds originally scattered over 30,000 acres of prairies, most of those not already leveled by plows and cows and bulldozers were, in the 1960s, being ravaged by

Aerial view of the "pimpled plain" of the Mima Mounds

motorcycle hoodlums. The Nature Conservancy, the National Park Service, and Evergreen State College stepped in; in the 1970s the State Department of Natural Resources assumed protection and management and interpretation.

Begin at the dome of the interpretive center. Study the displays, then walk the paved ½-mile self-guiding nature trail, consulting the pamphlet that explains the evolution of the plant community.

Next, wander the 3–4 miles of less formal trails any old way, any old how. The Natural Area Preserve, 445 acres, is thoroughly sampled—fields, forest, and clumps of shrub-like firs pioneering the fields. The cessation of regular burning by the Original Inhabitants, done prior to 1850 to perpetuate their "camas root farms," has resulted in expansion of forests. The spring flower show is famous—the grassland turns blue with camas blooms. In summer come the bluebells, wooly sunflowers, oxeye daisies. Even late October usually has a profusion of bluebells-of-Scotland amid the golden grass and the airy balls of yellow-green lichen. Birds: little flitterers in the grass seeking seeds and bugs, raptors patrolling above on the lookout for little critters in the grass.

And mounds. Some in the woods, covered with moss and ferns. Some in the prairies, covered with grass and herbs. Contrast those seen from highways, low bumps nearly or completely flattened, to those here, in full original relief.

Don't rush. Take your time. Feel the vibrations. Watch out for Ancient Astronauts.

BLACK HILLS CREST

Round trip: 8 miles
High point: 2667 feet
Elevation gain: 1100 feet
Map: 55

The two highest Black Hills, Capitol Peak and Big Larch Mountain, command a sweep of horizons—prairies, Whulge, Olympics, and five volcanoes. I favor Big Larch because on a crystalline day of late October I saw from there, for the first and only time in my travels of Whulge country, the white gleam deep in the Olympics that was unmistakably the veritable Olympus, and at the same time, as from a peak in Darien, waves of the Oceane Sea shining in the lowering sun. Boy.

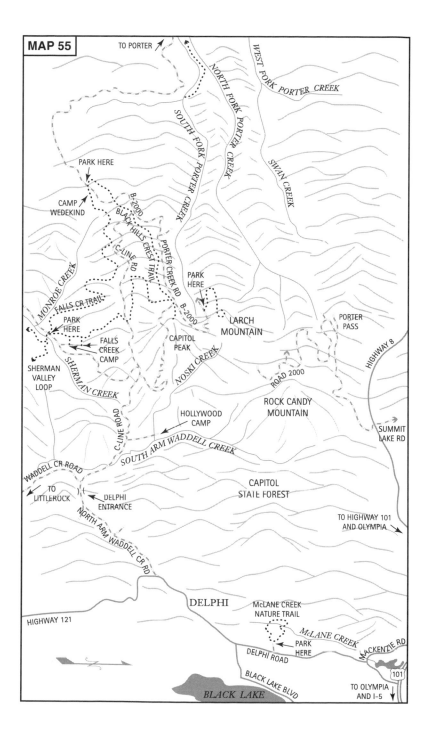

MAP 55

TO PORTER

WEST FORK PORTER CREEK

NORTH FORK PORTER CREEK

SOUTH FORK PORTER CREEK

SWAN CREEK

PARK HERE

CAMP WEDEKIND

B-2000

BLACK HILLS CREST TRAIL

C-LINE RD

PORTER CREEK RD

MONROE CREEK

FALLS CR TRAIL

PARK HERE

FALLS CREEK CAMP

SHERMAN VALLEY LOOP

SHERMAN CREEK

C-LINE ROAD

PARK HERE

B-2000

LARCH MOUNTAIN

PORTER PASS

HIGHWAY 8

CAPITOL PEAK

NOSKI CREEK

ROAD 2000

ROCK CANDY MOUNTAIN

SUMMIT LAKE RD

HOLLYWOOD CAMP

SOUTH ARM WADDELL CREEK

WADDELL CR ROAD

TO LITTLEROCK

DELPHI ENTRANCE

NORTH ARM WADDELL CR RD

CAPITOL STATE FOREST

TO HIGHWAY 101 AND OLYMPIA

DELPHI

McLANE CREEK NATURE TRAIL

McLANE CREEK

MACKENZIE RD

HIGHWAY 121

PARK HERE

DELPHI ROAD

101

TO OLYMPIA AND I-5

BLACK LAKE BLVD

BLACK LAKE

Stroll for miles in bilberry and bracken and alpine-seeming shrubby firs, the sky-surrounded crest eerily moor-like.

Then, on the brink of the plunge from the Black Hills to the Chehalis River, I looked across 2½ miles of emerald floodplain to the opposite side of the valley that was dug millennia ago by the Really Big River, several times the size of today's Columbia, the sum of all the rivers of the Cascades and Olympics dammed from more direct routes to the sea by the wall of Canadian ice.

These are two reasons I cannot cheerfully commend the Capitol State Forest and its Department of Natural Resources mismanagers to the attention of that loose asteroid we are promised by astronomers.

Directions: *Go off Exit 104 in Olympia and drive US 101 west 2 miles. Turn south at the exit signed "West Olympia, Black Lake," on Black Lake Boulevard 4 miles to a T with Delphi Road. Drive Delphi Road–Waddell Creek Road past the Delphi Entrance to a Y junction. Take the right fork 1.4 miles to a split. Go left on the C-Line Road, signed "Capitol Peak 9 miles." Stay with the C-Line Road 7 miles to a junction on the ridge crest, 2150 feet. Turn left on road No. B-2000 for 1.5 miles to Wedekind Pass, elevation 1896 feet.*

This five-star scenic supershow of the Black Hills ends atop Capitol Peak and has all those views. But in addition are kaleidoscopes from the trail along the crest of the range's longest, highest ridge, between the valleys of Sherman and Porter Creeks. Stroll for miles in bilberry and bracken and alpine-seeming shrubby firs, the sky-surrounded crest eerily moor-like. Enough to make a Scot homesick. Or an Ozark Mountain boy.

Follow the succession of "Capitol Peak" signs. Not that you can go wrong, there on the ridge crest. On wings, almost, liberated from heavy Earth, stroll a little up, a little down, from one "moor" to another. Grass and salal, huckleberry and salmonberry, old stumps and young firs, including plantations of alpine-appearing nobles. Lumps of weathered basalt columns poke through thin soil. In season the way is colorful with alpine-seeming flowers. Moors fall off right to Sherman Valley and Chehalis Valley draining to the ocean, left to Porter Valley and the lacework of blue inlets and green peninsulas of South Sound and the Great Bend of Hood Canal. Ahead are the stump ridge of Big Larch and the surreal summit towers of Capitol. Rainier looms whitely beyond.

Twice the road is crossed and twice more can be briefly glimpsed, but mostly the walker is totally unaware of wheels, so skillfully is the trail placed. The second crossing can confuse. This is at the 2150 foot saddle where the C-Line Road tops the ridge (see page 234). Take a few steps right from the junction along the C-Line Road and go left on a lesser road obscurely signed "Trail." In a couple hundred feet the trail indeed takes off up left to the crest. After a final grassy, rocky, meadow-like knoll at 2450 feet, the trail drops the short bit to a final 2150-foot saddle, that of Capitol Forest Vista, there meeting the upper end of the Capitol Peak Trail from Sherman Valley. The final ¾ miles is on the road to Capitol Peak, 2667 feet.

OTHER TRIPS

Deschutes Falls. This Thurston County park has 150 acres, a mile of Deschutes River frontage, the 75-foot-deep slot gorge, the waterfalls 15 and 35 feet high, grassy meadows, and riverbank ancient forest.

McLane Creek Nature Trail

Skookumchuck Falls. Walk past the closed Weyerhaeuser gates, cross the divide from the Deschutes to the Skookumchuck, proceed up the latter, and discover a splendid stretch of wild river tumbling over a series of cascades to a mini-canyon of mossy bedrock bright with columbine.

Bald Hill Lake Natural Area. The history of the area over the centuries was one of repeated fires, creating and perpetuating the "balds." Some 337 acres, including an unlogged canyon and the balds, here only lightly grazed, are managed by the State DNR as a Natural Area Preserve. Some thirty-five grasses have been found, half of them native. The display of ferns includes a number of the unusual and rare. More than 300 plants have been identified. Many are at their northern limits and remind of Oregon; many "don't belong" on this side of the Cascades and remind of eastern Washington.

McLane Creek Nature Trail (map 55). Beaver ponds, beaver dams, beaver lodges, and—if you're quiet and lucky—beaver splashing about their business oblivious to the audience. And an encyclopedia of woodland plants and marsh plants and swamp plants, on a mere 41 acres of DNR land that seem ten times that.

THE WESTERN SKYLINE

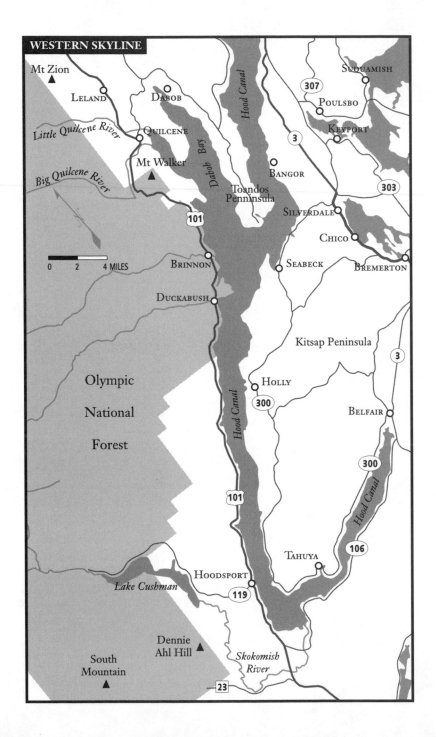

WESTERN SKYLINE

THE WESTERN SKYLINE

Management: U.S. Forest Service
Topographic maps: USGS Potlatch, The Brothers, Brinnon—
and their equivalents in the Green Trails series, privately
published

To look west from Puget Sound City is to see, to gaze upon, the Olympic Mountains. Were a person to look east from there to Puget Sound City, what would one see?

Though it's too distant from city homes for more than occasional day hikes, anybody who looks to the range very often must now and then go there to take a look from. Three peaks on or near the skyline, one at either end and one in the middle, are choice. The dead of winter or its edges are best, for the clarity of north-wind air and for the snowline-probing freedom from the wheel.

SOUTH MOUNTAIN

Round trip: (both peaks) 9½ miles
High point: 3125 feet
Elevation gain: 2175 feet
Map: 56

On the crystal-air November day of my first survey, I saw five volcanoes and one ocean, plus a Canal and a Sound and Three Fingers, Index, Phelps, Daniel, Chimney Rock, Goat Rocks, Green and Gold, Issaquah Alps, Doty and Bald and Black and Willapa Hills. South is the absolute southernmost peak of the Olympics, a unique viewpoint giving novel perspectives on the full length and width of the Puget Trough.

Directions: *Drive US 101 to 0.7 mile south of the Skokomish River*

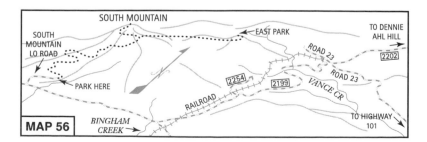

Olympic Mountains from South Mountain

and turn west on Skokomish Valley Road. At a Y in 6 miles go right on road No. 23, signed "Dennie Ahl Seed Orchard." In 2.2 miles, where road No. 2202 turns right, continue straight on road No. 23, signed "Brown Creek Campground." In 0.2 mile turn left on road No. 2199. Round a promontory (look down to pastures at the upper limit of the Skokomish floodplain) and drop to cross Vance Creek. In 3.3 miles from the turn onto road No. 2199, road No. 2254 (not signed) and the abandoned railroad grade join in from the right. At 4.5 miles from road No. 23 is a T at Bingham Creek; go right and stay on the main road. At 2 miles from Bingham Creek is a side road right, perhaps inconspicuously signed "South Mountain 820." Turn up it, immediately starting to climb. In 0.5 mile is a big switchback. Park here, elevation 950 feet.

The road may be drivable beyond, all the way to the summit, and that's why wheel-stopping snowbanks are desirable. However, spring has the flowers and midweek is unlikely to have wheels. (Spring comes early on this south slope.) Views start almost immediately through windows in the second-growth and grow to wide-open panoramas. The busy, entertaining route winds into valleys and out on spurs, crosses saddles, cuts through walls of rubbly basalt and harder pillow lava. Flower gardens on walls and in creeklets compete for attention—

fields of lupine and beargrass are especially striking. In 3 miles, at 2750 feet, is a saddle in the summit ridge, adding views north. Left ½ mile is West Peak, 3125 feet, formerly a lookout site, now bare and lonesome. Right on an up-and-down ridge crest 1¼ miles is radio-towered East Peak, 3000 feet.

Flower gardens on walls and in creeklets compete for attention—fields of lupine and beargrass are especially striking.

Here on the scarp that without prelude leaps up 2000 feet are views that demand large-area maps and long hours. Close at hand, of course, are Olympics: a foreground of ridges and valleys denuded of trees, one of the most surrealistic scenes of clearcutting in all the Northwest; footstool peaks, Dennie Ahl and Dow; and the rugged heights, The Brothers, Washington, Ellinor, Pershing, Copper, and Cruiser. The East Peak (this is the one you see while driving up the Skokomish) gives the classic look down to the pastured floodplain of the valley curving around to join Hood Canal at the Great Bend. The West Peak (whose basalt surprisingly is capped by conglomerate) gives the dramatic vista to Grays Harbor. Below south is the forest plateau of the glacier terminus. Beyond this gulf where the meltwater streams flowed, including the Pretty Big River of ice-dammed rivers from the east side of the Olympics, rise the Black Hills, beyond which rolled the Really Big River from the Cascades; beyond that valley (now the Chehalis) are the Doty and Willapa Hills. Close enough below to see the house the Spring twins grew up in is Shelton, mills pluming.

For purposes of this book Ira and Pat Spring spent the night on the summit, viewing lights from Aberdeen to Olympia to Everett, and he was so knocked out that when the sun came up he forgot to take a picture.

MOUNT WALKER

Round trip: (trail) 5 miles
High point: 2804
Elevation gain: (trail) 2100 feet
Map: 57

Directions: *Drive US 101 to the Mount Walker Viewpoint road, No. 2730, at Walker Pass, 5 miles south of Quilcene. Elevation, 727 feet.*

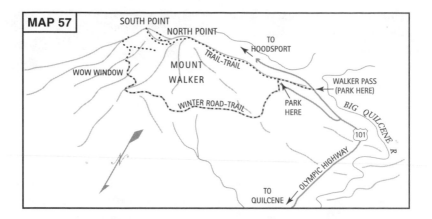

The absolute easternmost summit of the Olympics, zapping straight up from Hood Canal, sitting out by its lonesome, cut off from neighbors by a deep glacier trough, Walker is, apart from skyline peaks, the most prominent point in the range as seen from Seattle. It follows that from Walker one can readily see Seattle—and all the other neighborhoods of Puget Sound City and everything in between. The only thing wrong is a road to the top. On second consideration, that's not so wrong. In winter (October through April), the road is gated at the highway and thus is a trail. In other seasons there is the other and veritable trail.

The trail was there before the road but for some years was lost in the brush before volunteers came a-whacking. Views are less plentiful than on the road-trail. But the distance is less, by half. Wheels are banned. In June you may go blind from the color show.

Drive a scant 0.2 mile up from the highway to the clearly marked trailhead, elevation 775 feet. The path ascends steeply, unpleasantly so under a boot-depth of snow, and is so slippery when wet that many hikers then prefer to ascend the trail and descend the road. But in rhododendron time! As the feet move slowly up the trail, the nose is thrusting through masses of blossoms.

At 1½ miles, 2450 feet, the trail switchbacks over a large rock outcrop. At the top is a vista of Buck, Turner, Crag, Constance, Warrior, Buckhorn, and Townsend. The trail comes out at North Point, 2804 feet, just west of where the lookout tower used to be. The views from the basalt garden are enormous over Walker Pass to the Big Quilcene valley and Constance, north to Zion and San Juan Islands and Canada.

A scant ½ mile away, at 2750 feet, is South Point Observation.

Canada Jay, commonly called Camp Robber, on Mount Walker

The foreground is saltwater at the foot of the mountain—Quilcene Bay off Dabob Bay off Hood Canal. The middleground is the Kitsap Peninsula. The background: Cascades from Baker to Glacier to Rainier to St. Helens; cities and towns from Everett to Seattle to Bremerton to Tacoma. Look at a map of Whulge country—whatever is on the map you probably can see from Walker.

MOUNT ZION

Round trip: 4 miles
High point: 4273 feet
Elevation gain: 1400 feet
Map: 58

The summit is too high and the miles of high road to the trailhead too many for this to be a convenient snowline-prober except in late spring, but it only takes a couple of snowbanks to stop the wheels someplace along the way, in timely season for early flowers, at least.

Directions: *From US 101 at 2 miles north of Quilcene, take the paved*

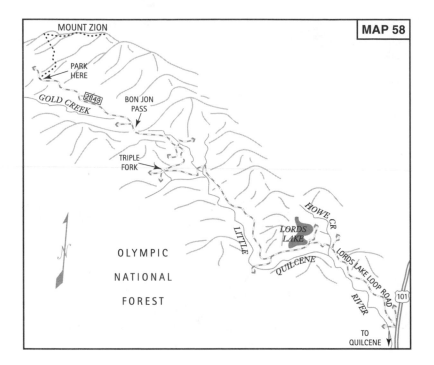

Lords Lake Loop Road. In 3.4 miles, just below the (Port Townsend) reservoir dam, go left on a gravel road signed "Mt. Zion Trail 7, Little Quilcene Trail 9." In 4.2 more miles is a triple fork; keep right, signed "Mt. Zion Trail 3," in views down the Little Quilcene valley to the end of Quilcene Bay. In 1.2 miles, at Bon Jon Pass, 2900 feet, take a right, contouring the northeast side of Gold Creek valley. At 2 miles from the pass, 11.2 miles from US 101, is the trailhead, elevation 2900 feet.

An "island mountain" cut off from the main range by deep valleys dating from the Ice Age, Zion is a very high peak to be stuck so far out in lowlands. There's absolutely nothing to block the view from Seattle to Vancouver. See mountains of Vancouver Island, waterways of Whulge far south on Puget Sound and north on the Strait of Georgia, Cascades from Rainier to Baker. Turn west to see the Dungeness River valley, Graywolf Ridge, and, over Bon Jon Pass and the head of the Little Quilcene River, Mount Townsend. Look down to Port Discovery close below, to see the fish jumping.

> *Look down to Port Discovery close below, to see the fish jumping.*

The 4723-foot summit was burned bare by the 1916 forest fire and remains wide-open, all trees diminutive, and in early summer the flower show is brilliantly subalpine. Sit on a bald-rock knob at the site of the long-gone lookout cabin and immerse yourself in the big picture. On my first visit all I saw was the gleaming surface of a horizon-to-horizon cloudsea, through which poked just the tip of my island. Not bad.

OTHER TRIPS

Big Quilcene Lookout. The clear-cut site of the lookout, 3450 feet, is close enough to Mount Constance to see the mountain goats begging cookies from the mountain climbers, and Quilcene pastures are just a long moo away.

Webb Lookout. In a straight line with Green and Gold on the Kitsap Peninsula and the Issaquah Alps east of Seattle, this 2775-foot peak north of the Hamma Hamma River can be imagined to be a companion remnant of the Old (pre-Olympic and pre-Cascade) Mountains. The view is straight down to Hood Canal and out to everywhere.

Jorsted Point. The narrow, steep road to a 2300-foot helispot just south of the Hamma Hamma and close east of Washington and Pershing and hanging in the air above Hood Canal makes a fine and lonesome walk.

Dow Mountain. Cut off from neighbors by two deep valleys, the North Fork Skokomish drowned by Cushman Reservoir and a wind gap used in the long ago by ice and water, Dow is an island mountain, sensationally located close above Hood Canal beside the craggy mass of Washington. Do the road walk to the 2600-foot summit in winter, before blood stirs in the slugheads who come on sunny Sundays to racket on the mount.

Dennie Ahl Hill. On a crisp winter day when wheels are discouraged by snow, the walker can look out from the 2004-foot summit rising steeply above the Skokomish valley to three volcanoes and half a dozen cities and towns, plus ice-chiseled crags of high mountains and sparkling waves of low waters.

Skokomish Delta. The largest delta of the Hood Canal side of the Olympics is the wildest, the lonesomest, and most scenic. The preserve of solitude, nearly 3 miles wide and up to 2 miles deep from

The largest delta of the Hood Canal side of the Olympics is the wildest, the lonesomest, and most scenic.

saltwater to civilization, not counting a couple square miles of low-tide mudflats, give a walker plenty of space to commune with plovers and herons and clams and cows, and sniff the breezes blowing aromas of the saltmeadows that in spring are fields of flowers. Potlatch State Park lets feet on the beach ½ mile from the delta edge.

NORTHWARD HO!

When the distances from Hadrian's Wall to Persia, Sahara to Danube, became too great for a single emperor, the Roman Empire was divided between the imperiums of Rome and Constantinople. The map may say the distances from Bellingham to Tenino, Cascade front to Olympic front, are the same in 2002 as they were in 1976, when I began my survey of the "wildness within" the Puget Trough. That is because the map hasn't recently driven Interstate 5 between

Snohomish River from Lord Hill Regional Park

the north and south boundaries of my *Footsore* inventory, or tried getting from Cougar Mountain to Hood Canal and back in a single day.

I hope the libraries have not tossed out my old editions, rather have moved them to the history department to keep company with Gibbon and Hobsbawm. In 1995 I retired the *Footsores* from the active political front in favor of a more selective inventory of much the same territory (except the shores of the Whulge, which were brought together in a single volume, *Walks and Hikes on Beaches Around Puget Sound*).

Fortunately, Ken Wilcox, my fellow member of the board of directors of the North Cascades Conservation Council, began walking-writing-publishing his County Series, volumes on Snohomish, Skagit, and Whatcom Counties and the San Juan Islands. These are not in the genus of the new generation of cream-skimmers inspired by the vision of easy money, but honorable companions of the Spring-Manning guidebooks that are done to advance the preservation of wildness through the publicizing of trails and thus the green-bonding and recruitment of new feet.

So, in warm gratitude I cede to him my erstwhile northern domains of "wildness within" between the saltchuck and the ice. In his books you will find (amid much else) the following, a few of my favorite things:

Lord Hill Regional Park, a little sibling of the Issaquah Alps.

Wallace Falls State Park, proposed to be expanded in a superpark extending to the summit ridge of Stickney and east to May Creek.

West Fork Miller River, Sierra-like white water tumbling over granite slabs, a finger of "Management Zone" intruding the Alpine Lakes Wilderness.

Silver Creek, original route of prospectors rushing to stake claims in the treasure trove thought to be "as rich as Monte Cristo."

"Whulge-to-Whitehorse Trail" (North Fork Stillaguamish River), on old rail grade from Port Susan to Darrington.

Fire Mountain (Cultus Mountain) and "Wickersham-Woolley-Lyman Mountain," the pair of 4000-foot behemoths that hulk above the Skagit Delta.

Devil's Garden, a jumble of monster boulders that tumbled onto the Canadian glacier from Fire Mountain and were carried south several miles before the ice melted away beneath them.

North Cascades Corridor, which Ken and company are proposing be created between the Nooksack and Skagit Rivers, hitching the saltwater to the glaciers of Mount Baker.

Larrabee State Park, encompassing Chuckanut Mountain, where the Cascade scarp plunges to the beaches.

Elephant Mountain (Blanchard Hill) Natural Resources Conservation Area, another proposal where Ken is a leader, encompassing the renowned Oyster Dome and the Bat Caves.

Devil's Garden

INDEX

ABOUT THE AUTHOR

Harvey Manning, a student then an instructor in the club's Climbing Course, was delegated in 1954 to prepare a new textbook. In 1960 he and the committee of editors he chaired produced *Mountaineering: The Freedom of the Hills*, now known around much of the world simply (and reverently) as *Freedom*. Profits, substantial because the editors and writers received no royalties, provided the wherewithal for a Literary Fund. In the dozen years of Manning's chairmanship of the managing committee (proud to be sneered at as "the amateurs"), it founded a "company" (Mountaineers Books), whose publications included Tom Miller's *The North Cascades*, which was America's introduction to the continent's iciest wilderness south of the 49th parallel; Dee Molenaar's classic *Challenge of Rainier*; Brock Evans' *Alpine Lakes* (the book that made President Ford proud to sign the bill establishing the Alpine Lakes Wilderness); and other volumes serving the club's purposes announced in 1906. Best known is the *100 Hikes* series; after turning the Literary Fund Committee over to "the professionals," Manning became the partner of Ira Spring as co-author of guidebooks.

With his daughter Penny he did a book (this one) on "the wilderness within" and a companion on walking the beaches, stressing the necessity of defending the Public Trust Doctrine, which declares that there is no such a thing as a private beach, against the privatizing done through the Private Greed Doctrine. His interests having shifted from wilderness climbing to wilderness preservation, he was elected to the

Harvey Manning soaking his blistered feet after walking 3,000 miles exploring the beaches and winter trails

board of directors of the North Cascades Conservation Council, the spearhead group that led the way to victory in the campaign for a North Cascades National Park. His wife Betty is editor of the organization's thrice-yearly publication, *The Wild Cascades*, "the thinking person's preservation journal." The organization has published the history written for it by Manning, *Conservation and Conflict: The U.S. Forest Service and National Park Service in the North Cascades, 1892– 1992*, which sets the record straight on matters that are still being obfuscated by the opponents of wilderness and the "mugwimp" wing of wilderness advocacy. For the Sierra Club, Manning wrote (on command of the late Dave Brower) one of Dave's historic Exhibit Formats, *The Wild Cascades: Forgotten Parkland;* with Tom Miller's book, this delivered the one-two punch that helped win the North Cascades Act of 1968.

On the local scale, Manning is infamous among teeth-gnashing land-developers for creating (naming, that is) the Issaquah Alps. During his (founding) presidency of the Issaquah Alps Trails Club, King County created the Cougar Mountain Regional Wildland Park, the nation's largest urban wildland (wheelfree, that is) park and Washington state established the West Tiger Mountain Natural Resources Conservation Area, administered under the state's version of the national Wilderness Act. Manning's *Walking the Beach to Bellingham* (not a guidebook, thank heaven, but a personal memoir of doing it) was reissued in 2002.